MW00425866

About the ITSM Library

The publications in the ITSM Library cover best practice in IT management and are published on behalf of itSMF International.

The IT Service Management Forum (itSMF) is the association for IT service organizations, and for customers of IT services. itSMF's goal is to promote innovation and support of IT management. Suppliers and customers are equally represented within the itSMF. The Forum's main focus is exchange of peer knowledge and experience. Our authors are global experts.

The following publications are, or soon will be, available.

Introduction, Foundations and Practitioners books
- Foundations of IT Service Management based on ITIL® (V2, Arabic, Chinese, German, English, French, Italian, Japanese, Korean, Dutch, Brazilian Portuguese, and Russian; Danish and Spanish)
- Foundations of IT Service Management based on ITIL® (V3, English, Dutch)
- IT Service Management - An Introduction (V2, being replaced by V3, only a few languages left)
- IT Service Management - An Introduction (V3, English, Dutch)
- IT Services Procurement based on ISPL - An Introduction (Dutch)
- Project Management based on PRINCE2™ 2005 Edition (Dutch, English, German)
- Release & Control for IT Service Management, based on ITIL® - A Practitioner Guide (English)

IT Service Management - best practices
- IT Service Management - best practices, part 1 (Dutch)
- IT Service Management - best practices, part 2 (Dutch)
- IT Service Management - best practices, part 3 (Dutch)
- IT Service Management - best practices, part 4 (Dutch)

Topics & Management instruments
- Metrics for IT Service Management (English)
- Six Sigma for IT Management (English)
- The RfP for IT Outsourcing - A Management Guide (Dutch)
- Service Agreements - A Management Guide (English)
- Frameworks for IT Management (English, German, Japanese)
- IT Governance based on CobiT® - A Management Guide (English, German)

Pocket guides
- IT Service Management - A summary based on ITIL® (V2, Dutch)
- IT Service Management - A Pocket Guide (V3, English, Dutch)
- IT Service Management based on ITIL - A Pocket Guide (V3, English, Dutch)
- IT Service Management from Hell!! (V2, English)
- IT Service Management from Hell. Based on Not-ITIL (V3, English)
- ISO/IEC 20000 - A Pocket Guide (English, German, Japanese, Italian, Spanish, formerly BS 15000 - A Pocket Guide)
- IT Services Procurement based on ISPL - A Pocket Guide (English)
- IT Service CMM - A Pocket Guide (English)
- Six Sigma for IT Management - A Pocket Guide (English)
- Frameworks for IT Management - A Pocket Guide (English, Dutch)

For any further enquiries about ITSM Library, please visit www.itsmfbooks.com, http://en.itsmportal.net/en/books/itsm_library or www.vanharen.net.

Frameworks for IT Management
A POCKET GUIDE

*it*SMF **International**
The IT Service Management Forum

A publication of itSMF International

Colophon

Title:	Frameworks for IT Management - A Pocket Guide
A publication of:	itSMF International
Authors & editors:	Eric Rozemeijer (lead author, Quint Wellington Redwood)
	Jan van Bon (chief editor ITSM Library, Inform-IT)
	Tieneke Verheijen (editor, Inform-IT)
Publisher:	Van Haren Publishing, Zaltbommel, www.vanharen.net, for itSMF International
ISBN(13):	987 90 8753 087 7
Edition:	First edition, first impression, September 2007
Design & Layout:	CO2 Premedia, Amersfoort – NL
Printer:	Wilco, Amersfoort – NL

TRADEMARK NOTICES
PRINCE2™, M_o_R® and ITIL® are Registered Trade Marks and Registered Community Trade Marks of the Office of Government Commerce, and are Registered in the U.S. Patent and Trademark Office.
COBIT® is a registered trademark of the Information Systems Audit and Control Association (ISACA)/IT Governance Institute (ITGI).
The PMBoK® is a registered trademark of the Project Management Institute (PMI).
eTOM® is a registered trademark of the TeleManagement Forum.

Foreword

IT managers today are confronted with an overwhelming number of management frameworks, methods and methodologies – so many in fact that sometimes it's difficult to see the wood for the trees. Also, many IT service providers believe they can't be taken seriously if they don't also offer their own unique framework – which makes it even more difficult to find your way through the framework forest.

In general, management frameworks focus on quality. Applying standardized practices, and providing models that reflects these practices in a comprehensive way, has been a valuable aid to business managers for a long time. IT managers are no different. In addition, the field of Information Technology has always been deeply involved with modeling, simply because all development projects start with a model. Both factors help explain why the IT discipline has so many frameworks on offer.

But how do you chose the right framework from this huge range? Or maybe you need more then one, since they all tend to serve different goals…? Should you create your own framework by recombining elements from existing ones? Questions like these have been on the agenda of IT managers for decades.

This itSMF publication covers the most important frameworks in use for quality management in IT organizations. The descriptions are provided in a neutral and objective way, so that readers can gain a better understanding the potential value of each instrument. A consistent approach to each chapter allows easy comparison between the frameworks: a short profile, a description and core graphics, and the relevance to IT management are provided for each framework.

This first edition of the frameworks pocket guide contains descriptions of (in alphabetical order) AS 8015, ASL, BiSL, CMMI, CobiT, EFQM, eSCM-SP, eTOM, Generic Framework for Information Management, IPMA Competence Baseline, ISO 15504, ISO 19770, ISO/IEC 20000, ISO 27001, ISO 9000, ISPL, IT Balanced Scorecard, ITIL (V2 and V3), M_o_R, MSP, PMBoK, PRINCE2, Six Sigma, TickIT, TOGAF, and TQM, and is largely based on the introduction-level title "Frameworks for IT Management" in the ITSM Library.

The frameworks are categorized according to their main goal, and each framework is plotted against the largest and broadest 'umbrella' framework available, the 3x3 matrix for Information Management. This categorization should support the reader in finding the most suitable frameworks for their situation.

New frameworks will be added to this pocket guide, when they attract the attention of IT service managers, or grow in importance. This will make the pocket guide a living document, reflecting the actual situation in the field. The resulting frameworks pocket guide is a reliable and consistent reference guide, whether it is used as a first introduction to frameworks you haven't seen before, or as a quick reference guide to the core information on the frameworks you already know. In all cases the pocket guide should provide a valuable information source for modern IT managers. We hope it will support you in meeting the high demands of modern IT Service Management.

Jan van Bon,
Chief Editor ITSM Library for itSMF International

Acknowledgements

This pocket guide is largely based on the Introduction-level book "Frameworks for IT Management", a very succesful title in the ITSM Library. The scope of the pocket guide differs at some points from this larger title, based on the fact that some IT Service Management examination requirements have required us to cover some additional frameworks and standards.

We wish to thank lead-author Eric Rozemeijer (Quint Wellington Redwood), who not only created the management level summaries on the frameworks that were covered in the existing larger title, but who also covered the frameworks and standards that were subsequently added. The new sections were drafted using the same structure as used for all the other chapters, creating a consistent pocket guide.

The text of this pocket guide was originally part of the upgraded ITSM Library title "IT Service Management - An Introduction", published in September 2007. Based on the high level of interest in frameworks it was decided to also publish the text in a separate cover, as a pocket guide.

This pocket guide is largely based on the content of the larger Frameworks book. The authors of that book have therefore been fundamental to the creation of this title and we wish to thank them again for their contributions to the itSMF best practice series:
• Samantha Alford (ISO 9000 chapter)
• Rolf Akker (Generic Framework for Information Management chapter)
• Raul Assaff (PMBoK chapter)
• Colin Bentley (PRINCE2 chapter)
• Jacqueline van der Bent (TQM chapter)
• Paul Breslin (TickIT chapter)
• Marghanita da Cruz (AS 8015 chapter)
• Ralph Donatz (BiSL chapter, together with Frank van Outvorst)

- Rubina Faber (M_o_R chapter)
- Edgar Giesen (Six Sigma chapter, together with Patrick Teters)
- Wim van Grembergen (IT Balanced Scorecard chapter, together with Steven de Haes)
- Steven De Haes (IT Balanced Scorecard chapter, together with Wim van Grembergen)
- Jon G. Hall (ISO 27001 chapter)
- Bert Hedeman (MSP chapter)
- Jan Hendriks (eTOM chapter)
- Peter Hill (CobiT chapter)
- Majid Iqbal (eSCM chapter, together with Mark Paulk)
- Gerrit Koch (IPMA representative for PMI-Netherlands, ICB chapter)
- Ivor Macfarlane (ISO 20000 chapter)
- Dr Machteld Meijer (ASL chapter, together with Mark Smalley)
- Gianluca Mulè (EFQM chapter)
- Dr Frank Niessink (IT Service CMM chapter)
- Dr Mark Paulk (eSCM chapter, together with Majid Iqbal)
- Colin Rudd (ITIL chapter)
- Mark Smalley (ASL chapter, together with Machteld Meijer)
- Frank van Outvorst (BiSL chapter, together with Ralph Donatz)
- Patrick Teters (Six Sigma chapter, together with Edgar Giesen)
- Dr T.F. (Denis) Verhoef (ISPL chapter)
- Kobi Vider (CMMI chapter)

The quality review of this pocket guide was part of the review of the larger IT Service Management Introduction title. The review - as usual - was extensive and provided the editorial team with valuable improvements on the manuscript. We wish to thank these reviewers for their contributions to the Introduction book and to the text of this derived Frameworks pocket guide in particular:
- John van Beem, ISES International, Netherlands
- Aad Brinkman, Apreton, Netherlands
- Peter Brooks, PHMB Consulting, itSMF South Africa

- Rob van der Burg, Microsoft, Netherlands
- Judith Cremers, Getronics PinkRoccade Educational Services, Netherlands
- Rosario Fondacaro, Quint Wellington Redwood, Italy
- Peter van Gijn, LogicaCMG, Netherlands
- Jan Heunks, ICT Partners, Netherlands
- Linh Ho, Compuware Corporation, USA
- Kevin Holland, NHS, UK
- Ton van der Hoogen, ToTZ Diensten, Netherlands
- Matiss Horodishtiano, Amdocs, itSMF Israel
- Wim Hoving, BHVB, Netherlands
- Brian Johnson, CA, USA
- Kirstie Magowan, itSMF New Zealand
- Steve Mann, OpSys - SM2, itSMF Belgium
- Reiko Morita, Ability InterBusiness Solutions, Inc., Japan
- Jürgen Müller, Marval, Netherlands
- Ingrid Ouwerkerk, Getronics PinkRoccade Educational Services, Netherlands
- Ton Sleutjes, CapGemini, Netherlands
- Maxime Sottini, Innovative Consulting, itSMF Italy
- Patricia Speltincx, OpSys, Belgium
- Takashi Yagi, Hitachi Ltd., itSMF Japan

Complex projects like these, which involve a large number of people, need professional project management if they are to deliver a quality product. Once again I am indebted to Tieneke Verheijen, the Editor, who also managed the larger Frameworks title, who has ensured that another quality title could be added to the ITSM Library.

Given the desire for a broad consensus in the field of IT Service Management, new developments, additional material and other contributions from IT Service Management professionals are welcome to extend and further improve this publication. Any forwarded material will be discussed by the editorial team and where appropriate incorporated into new editions. Comments can be sent to the chief editor, email: j.van.bon@ inform-it.org.

Jan van Bon
Chief editor ITSM Library, for itSMF International

Contents

1 Introduction to frameworks

Any organization that delivers IT services to their customers with a goal to support the business processes, needs some sort of structure to achieve it. Historically, this structure was based around functions and technical capabilities. Currently, with the ever-increasing speed of changes, and the need for flexibility, this is no longer an option. Increasingly the structure is formed around processes and customers, just as in any other part of the organization. This is further supported by the requirement to be able to demonstrate effective processes and controls in the delivery of IT, to support the demands of regulatory requirements, such as Sarbanes-Oxley.

For these reasons, IT organizations are eager to embrace frameworks and standards that claim to make this possible. Some examples include:
• TQM for process orientation and continuous improvement
• CobiT for increased control
• CMMI for process control in software (and system) development
• ITIL version 2 for process control in operational and tactical services provisioning

Using and implementing these frameworks, IT organizations hope to be able to capture and manage the complexity of tomorrow's business in IT, and to meet regulatory requirements.

With the growing number of frameworks, covering various domains of IT management (eg service management, development management, procurement, strategy, information management, etc.) the coherence between the domains seems to suffer. The overall picture, that is so essential to provide end-to-end services across the domains, is getting less attention. Most frameworks focus on the tight relationship between processes within a certain domain. There are only a few frameworks that cover all domains, and even if they do, as a consequence, they seem to lack integration and/or they seem to be too high level to provide sufficient added value. There are a small number of examples where a framework seems to combine all desired aspects, but the proprietary framework is only made fully available to the clients of a particular consulting company, and is either not, or only partly, published.

Effective IT Service Management can only be achieved when both the cohesion of processes within a domain and the inter-domain dependencies are understood. Therefore, to provide effective service management we must especially understand the relevance and the interdependencies of all domains involved. After all, the customer is only interested in the end-results of the service provider's efforts.

2 Inventory of relevant frameworks

There are several sources of practical guidance to IT Service Management. Among these are ITIL and ISO/IEC 20000, but there are many other useful standards, best practices and frameworks available, from various sources.

There are many ways to categorize the frameworks currently available. Obviously none of them would do justice to all of the frameworks at hand. However, for the purpose of this Pocket Guide, we have categorized them by looking at their strongest focus, based on how and where the frameworks are used. This is illustrated in Table 1.

Category	Type	Frameworks
Quality Management and Business Process Management	Frameworks that focus on quality standards, applied to specific IT domains (services, security, development, architecture, general)	TQM
		EFQM
		ISO 9000
		ISO/IEC 20000
		TOGAF™
		TickIT
		ISO/IEC 19770
		ISO/IEC 15504
		ISO/IEC 27001
Quality Improvement	Frameworks that focus on assessment and improvement of processes, performance or other, not focusing on how-to aspects of operating the IT	CMMI
		Six Sigma
		eSCM-SP
		IT Balanced Scorecard

(Continued)

Category	Type	Frameworks
IT Governance	Frameworks that focus on how to organize the IT function in terms of responsibilities, controls, organization	AS 8015
		CobiT®
		M_O_R®
Information Management	Frameworks that focus on how to perform and organize certain aspects of information management, such as procurement, service delivery, requirements	Generic Framework for Information Management
		ITIL®
		BiSL
		ISPL
		eTOM®
		ASL
Project Management	Frameworks that focus on project, program and portfolio management, not specifically IT	MSP
		PRINCE2TM
		PMBoK®
		IPMA Competence Baseline

Table 1 Categorization of management frameworks

3 How can frameworks be applied in IT Service Management

The increasing amount of theory and knowledge on IT management has led to the development and the deployment of numerous frameworks. Most of the frameworks are rich in knowledge, contain a body of valuable practical experience and provide many learning opportunities for organizations. In practice however, not all organizations are able to benefit from the available knowledge and experience inherent to these frameworks.

There are several reasons for this:

- **Fit and Overlap** - Most frameworks focus on a particular domain of the information management function. ITIL focuses on service management, BiSL addresses information management, ASL addresses application management, CMMI concentrates on development, while ISPL is focused on supplier management, etc. The frameworks do not fit seamlessly together and there is overlap. For example, BiSL, ASL and ITIL feature similar processes. Applying frameworks to several domains without sub optimization requires a lot of co-ordination and alignment, which is difficult to achieve across domains without having an all-integrating framework at hand. As a result, it is not uncommon for organizations to apply a single framework to all domains of the information management function, thereby missing certain domain-specific aspects.

- **Linkage between the domains** - Most models focus on a particular aspect of ICT (service) management. All-integrating commercial frameworks solve this problem; however, they have only been partly published, and are not fully publicly available. It seems that, with the increasing knowledge about specific domains, the required integration between the domains does not get the attention it deserves. In other words, there are numerous detailed and valuable frameworks that describe sets of processes within a domain, but the scope of the processes seldom covers the full scope of IT management.

- **Compliancy Requirements** - Many organizations are now confronted with high compliancy requirements. The CoBiT framework supports organizations in meeting compliancy requirements. In fact, some organizations are regularly audited on CoBiT compliance. In practice, many organizations find it difficult to handle the complex relationships between eg CoBiT and some of the best practice frameworks (such as ITIL, CMMI or ISPL).

- **Lack of Business Focus** - Most frameworks tend to focus on (delivery) processes, not on (business) value and/or outcomes. They focus strongly on running the IT delivery function and adopt the inside-out perspective common for IT. This tends to divert the focus of many IT organizations from what really matters to the customers and the business.

- **Religion** - Frameworks which were developed for a specific management domain are sometimes 'lived' in an overly fanatic, and almost religious, way. The Framework then tends to become a purpose in itself, instead of a means to an end. Misuse of the framework, and/or application to a domain for which it was never developed, can then be the result, again losing focus for business added value.

In conclusion:

> Commonly and publicly available frameworks do not fit together like a simple jigsaw puzzle. They were created by different people, at different times, in different places, in different ways, for different reasons, focusing on different lifecycle phases/functions, processes, deliverables /aspects/outcomes, with different degrees of granularity, precision, quality and consistency. Having an integrated picture at hand that can act like an umbrella for all relevant frameworks is essential to help an organization successfully implement multiple frameworks.

So how are organizations to make maximum use of the available industry best practices?

4

Frameworks for IT Management – A Pocket Guide

4 An 'umbrella framework' for Information Management

The Generic Framework for Information Management (discussed in Section 22) can serve as an 'umbrella framework'. It can be used to position the other frameworks described in this Pocket Guide at the highest possible level, using the scope of the entire information management function (Figure 1a-e).

4.1 Quality Management and Business Process Management

Quality management and Business Process Management frameworks (Figure 1a):

- **TQM** - TQM is a complete management vision on quality management. TQM can be positioned at the strategic, tactical and operational level of the Business, Information and Technology domains.
- **EFQM** - The EFQM Excellence Model is a key framework for helping organizations in their drive towards excellence and more competitiveness, and involves all levels and domains of the umbrella framework.
- **ISO 9000** - ISO 9000:2000 is not restricted to any particular layer of management and can therefore can be used at all levels and domains of the umbrella framework.
- **ISO/IEC 20000** - This ISO standard can be used at the tactical and operational level of the Technology domain and partly in the Information domain.
- **TOGAF** - TOGAF is a framework for developing an enterprise architecture and can be positioned on the tactical level of the umbrella framework.

- **TickIT** - TickIT can be used to support the development of all types of software and can be positioned at the operational level of the Technology domain.
- **ISO/IEC 19770** - This ISO standard describes the processes and procedures of software asset management and can be positioned at the operational level of the Technology domain.
- **ISO/IEC 15504** - ISO/IEC 15504 is a framework for the assessment of software processes and can be applied in the operational level of the Technology domain.
- **ISO/IEC 27001** - Information management is also about information security. Determining the necessary level of information security, planning to implement, and pursuing the right level of information security, are important issues in information management. ISO/IEC 27001 can be positioned at the strategic, the tactical and the operational level in the Information domain of the umbrella framework.

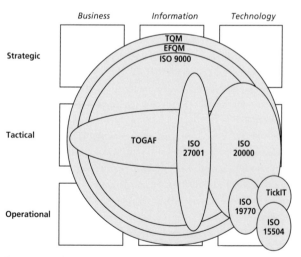

Figure 1a Cross-references for quality management and Business Process Management frameworks

4.2 Quality Improvement

Quality improvement frameworks (Figure 1b):

- **CMMI** - CMMI is focused on software development and maintenance processes, and covers the tactical and operational level of the Technology domain.

- **Six Sigma** - Six Sigma (6σ) is a structured, disciplined, rigorous approach to process improvement that can be positioned at the operational and tactical level of the Business, Information and Technology domains.

- **eSCM-SP** - The eSCM-SP will be useful to service organizations seeking to evaluate, develop and improve their capabilities in the design, deployment and delivery of IT-enabled services, as well as helping them manage risks associated with sourcing contracts during the initiation and completion phases. So it can be used at the tactical level of the Information and Technology domains.

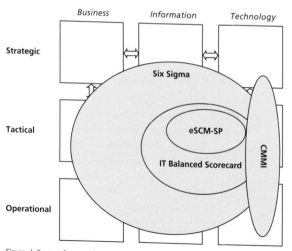

Figure 1b Cross-references for quality improvement frameworks

- **IT Balanced Scorecard** - The IT Balanced Scorecard is an instrument that can be leveraged to measure and manage IT performance, and to enable alignment between the business and IT. Therefore it can be positioned at the tactical level of the Information and Technology domains.

4.3 IT Governance

IT Governance frameworks (Figure 1c):
- **AS 8015** - AS 8015-2005 provides a framework that directors of any organization can use to govern effectively the use of IT within their organization. It is positioned in the Business domain at tactical level.
- **CoBiT®** - CoBiT® enables clear policy development and good practice for IT control throughout organizations. Because CoBiT covers both the Information and the Technology domain, it can be used at the strategic and tactical levels of these domains.
- **M_o_R®** - 'Management of Risk' involves all the activities required to identify and control the exposure to risk that may have an impact on the business. Strategic, tactical and operational activities are required in the Information and Technology domains.

4.4 Information Management

Information management frameworks (Figure 1d):
- **Generic Framework for Information Management** - This framework consists of three domains through which information problems can be considered: Business, Information and Technology. There are also three levels: a strategic, tactical and operational layer. It is a model for interrelating the different components of information management. This model serves as the umbrella framework.
- **ITIL® version 2** - ITIL version 2 is primarily known as the ITIL Service Support and ITIL Service Delivery books; ITIL belongs to the Technology domain. From the two core books, ITIL Service Delivery can be positioned mainly at the tactical level and ITIL Service Support mainly at the operational level.

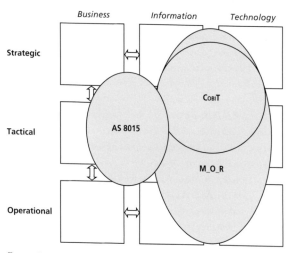

Figure 1c Cross-references for IT Governance frameworks

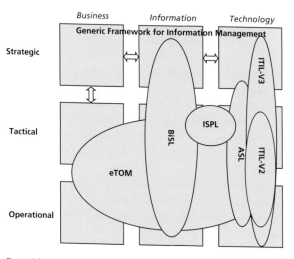

Figure 1d Cross-references for information management frameworks

- **ITIL® version 3** - ITIL version 3 covers the strategic, tactical and operational level and can be positioned at all three levels of the Technology domain.
- **BiSL** - BiSL can be positioned at the strategic, tactical and operational level of the Information domain, because it manages the functionality of the information processing functions for the business processes.
- **ISPL** - The Information Services Procurement Library (ISPL) is a practical approach to the procurement of IT services in the broadest sense of the word. This instrument can be used at the tactical level of the Information and Technology domains.
- **eTOM®** - The enhanced Telecom Operations Map (eTOM) is the most widely used and accepted standard for business process in the telecom industry. It can be positioned at the tactical and operational level of all three domains of the 'umbrella framework'.
- **ASL** - ASL offers a framework for application management. Because ASL covers the strategic, tactical and operational level, it can be positioned at all three levels of the Technology domain.

4.5 Project Management

Project management frameworks (Figure 1e):
- **MSP** - MSP describes how programs need to be carried out. It is an instrument that can be used on the tactical level of all three domains in the umbrella framework.
- **PMBoK®/PRINCE2TM/IPMA** - These methodologies describe how projects need to be carried out; they are instruments that can be used at the operational level of all three domains in the umbrella framework.

To achieve integration, overview and coherence between the different management domains and processes in this section, the CNIP principle can be used: *Co-operation when Necessary, Independent Operation when Possible.*

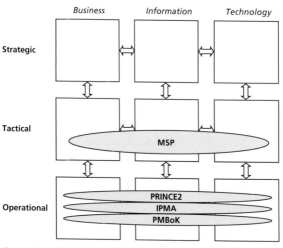

Figure 1e Cross-references for project management frameworks

Below, we offer three examples of integrating ITIL with other frameworks, namely COBIT, Six Sigma and CMMI:

Integrating ITIL with COBIT

ITIL focuses on efficiency and effectiveness of IT processes and managing the quality of IT services as perceived by the customer.

COBIT focuses on compliance of IT processes with relevant regulations, control over IT functions, consistency of outcomes, and managing risk ('define what you do, do what you say you do, and be able to produce evidence that you do it').

ITIL and CobiT can be used together to address the three primary aspects of IT governance:
- conformance
- performance
- relating responsibility

Use ITIL and CobiT together; ITIL for efficiency and effectiveness, CobiT for compliance and risk.
Use CobiT objectives as key metrics in a scorecard approach to report service performance.
Focus on the complementary nature of CobiT and ITIL.
ITIL service management maps to CobiT's Delivery & Support domain.
CobiT metrics are useful in SLA, OLA and UC specs.
ITIL provides process detail, complementary to CobiT.

Integrating ITIL with Six Sigma

ITIL specifies service processes, functions and techniques for managing IT services and IT infrastructure.

Six Sigma specifies a set of techniques for improving the quality of services and processes.

Many aspects of Six Sigma program and project guidance are applicable to ITIL:
- learning, knowledge transfer
- integrated management system
- fact/data-based decision-making
- use of technology tools
- defect removal focus

ITIL covers the process domain, Six Sigma covers the improvement method:
- ITIL requires a quality model like Six Sigma
- ITIL specifies core IT Service Management processes that can be subject to Six Sigma

Highlight how Six Sigma techniques are useful in:
- ongoing operation of ITIL processes
- business value-based project selection
- improvement projects

Integrating ITIL with CMMI

CMMI has a strong focus on the development of (new) services, while ITIL has a strong focus on managing the flawless integration of new services into the daily operations.

CMMI and ITIL both define and describe the change management process. In both frameworks this process is essential, providing an interface with the outside world.

In neither model is the relationship between these processes sufficiently described. Moreover, in most IT organizations completely separate project teams are responsible for implementing these processes, and these teams often do not communicate. As a result, the processes are designed and implemented without sufficient integration.

The focus of CMMI and ITIL initiatives should be on improvement within the respective development and operations organizations, as well as on improved co-operation between the two organizations. The most practical approach to this is by addressing issues and problems in a collaborative way. By leveraging the interfaces between development and operations, and promoting best practices like ITIL and CMMI in their respective areas, the organization can leverage expertise and experience from within (eg employee experiences and documented best practices) and from without (eg industry best practices).

5 Description of the frameworks

In the remainder of this Pocket Guide, we will describe the frameworks on a one-by-one basis. The order of presentation follows Table 1:

1. TQM - Total Quality Management
2. EFQM - the European Foundation for Quality Management Excellence Model
3. ISO/IEC 20000 - IT Service Management standard
4. ISO 9000 - Quality Management Systems
5. TOGAF™ - The Open Group Architecture Framework
6. TickIT - Quality management for IT
7. ISO/IEC 19770 - Software Asset Management (SAM)
8. ISO/IEC 15504 - also known as SPICE (Software Process Improvement and Capability dEtermination)
9. ISO/IEC 27001 - Information Security Management Systems
10. CMMI - Capability Maturity Model Integration
11. Six Sigma - statistical approach to quality improvement
12. eSCM-SP v2 - eSourcing Capability Model for Service Providers, version 2
13. IT Balanced Scorecard - the management system for strategic performance and results
14. AS 8015-2005 - Australian Standard for Corporate Governance of IT
15. CobiT - Control Objectives for Information and related Technologies
16. M_o_R - Management of Risk
17. Generic Framework for Information Management
18. ITIL - the IT Infrastructure Library (version 2 and 3)
19. BiSL - the Business Information Services Library
20. ISPL - the Information Services Procurement Library
21. eTOM - the enhanced Telecom Operations Map
22. ASL - the Application Services Library
23. MSP - Managing Successful Programmes

24. PRINCE2 - PRojects IN Changing Environments
25. PMBoK - the Project Management Body of Knowledge
26. IPMA Competence Baseline

Each framework is described in terms of:
- a short profile
- description and core graphics
- relevance to IT management

6 TQM – Total Quality Management

> *Total Quality Management (TQM) is a complete management vision in which everyone in the organization is continuously incentivized to fulfill the wishes of the internal and external customer, in order to reach a competitive advantage.*

6.1 Description and core graphics

Starting in the European and American industries, with the aim of catching up with Japanese competition in the 1970s and 1980s, TQM is now a worldwide recognized organizational change vision based on quality management. It is used in large and small profit and non-profit organizations.

TQM is not used as a single instrument. It is a collection of views and approaches on organizational change with related methodologies and techniques, all leading to a profound change in the way in which the organization is managed.

In general, management strives for a balance between high productivity, low cost and maximum profit. TQM is based upon this fundamental principle. To achieve this, TQM focuses on:
- statistical process control
- process management
- continuous improvement
- zero defects
- education and training
- the role of management
- teamwork

To keep the improvement process alive, customer and employee satisfaction, communication, deployment and cultural change are essential to achieve business excellence. One of the quality improvement techniques is The Deming Cycle, also known as the Plan-Do-Check-Act Cycle (in short, the P-D-C-A Cycle), see Figure 2.

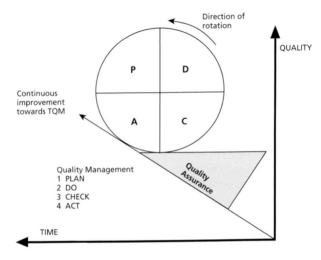

Figure 2 The P-D-C-A Cycle

Today, quality is no longer an issue for the central quality department manager alone, but for all management and employees. Line management in particular should show sufficient buy-in in order to stimulate all staff to follow their example. Quality can no longer be delegated. All aspects that are important to running a business, including mission, vision and strategy involvement of employees, entrepreneurship, process management, customer focus, working together with suppliers, continuous learning and business results, are part of TQM.

At the same time, TQM provides management with a set of tools and techniques to support the organization in the change process. When a clear business plan based on TQM is formulated and ready to implement in the organization, a range of methodologies and techniques are available to support the implementation process.

These techniques can be categorized as:
- leading change techniques, such as:
  - policy deployment
  - benchmarking
  - customer satisfaction surveys
  - employee motivation survey
  - managerial audits and self assessments (EFQM/MBNQA)
- process management techniques, specifically for:
  - development, for example Taguchi, Shainin
  - manufacturing, eg SPC, process capability, Six Sigma
  - logistics and supply management, eg Just-in-time, Kanban
- group dynamics, such as:
  - brainstorming
  - force field analysis
- problem solving:
  - Pareto diagram
  - cause and effect diagram

6.2 Relevance to IT management

IT policy is never a stand-alone policy, but is part of the policy of the organization. This sets the context for the IT policy, but new developments in IT can lead to other directions in the strategy of the organization. They influence each other. When getting the best out of both, they add value to the organization by improving efficiency, effectiveness and quality of processes: basic TQM principles.

Improving processes in an organization is very hard when the information on which decisions and subsequent initiatives are to be based is inaccurate and incomplete. The first product whose quality should be ensured is the management information: it serves all the other products and processes. This is why TQM is important for IT: it should ensure that information is reliable and safe.

7 EFQM – the European Foundation for Quality Management Excellence Model

The EFQM Excellence Model is a key framework for helping organizations in their drive towards excellence and more competitiveness. It is based on the premise that excellent results with respect to performance, customers, people and society are achieved through leadership driving policy and strategy, which is delivered through people, partnerships and resources.

7.1 Description and core graphics

The EFQM Excellence Model was introduced at the beginning of 1992 as the framework for assessing organizations for the EFQM Excellence Award and is now the most widely used organizational framework in Europe.

The EFQM has identified a number of Fundamental Concepts that it has used to underpin its successful management framework. These are:

- results orientation
- customers focus
- leadership & constancy of purpose
- management by processes & facts
- people development & involvement
- continuous learning, improvement & innovation
- partnership development
- corporate social responsibility

For an organization to maximize the benefits of adopting the EFQM Excellence Model, a management team must first ensure that it is comfortable with these Concepts. Clearly, if these Concepts are not fully understood and accepted, then progress with adopting the Model will be difficult and potentially meaningless. There is no significance related to the order of the Concepts. The list is not meant to be exhaustive and they will change as excellent organizations develop and improve.

7.1.1 The EFQM Excellence Model

The Model, which recognizes that there are many approaches to achieving sustainable excellence in all aspects of performance, is based on the premise that:

> Excellent results with respect to performance, customers, people and society are achieved through leadership driving policy and strategy that is delivered through people, partnerships and resources, and processes.

Figure 3 presents the EFQM Model. The arrows emphasize the dynamic nature of the Model. They show innovation and learning help to improve enablers that, in turn, lead to improved results.

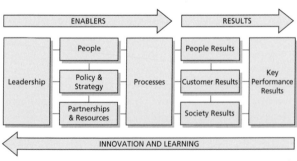

Figure 3 The EFQM Model (The EFQM Excellence Model is a registered trademark of EFQM)

The EFQM Model is a non-prescriptive framework based on nine criteria. Five of these criteria are 'enablers' (leadership, policy & strategy, people, partnership & resources and processes) and four are 'results' (customer results, people results, society results and key performance results). The 'enabler' criteria cover what an organization does. The 'results' criteria cover what an organization achieves. 'Results' are caused by 'enablers' and 'enablers' are improved using feedback from 'results'.

The EFQM Model's nine boxes represent the criteria against which to assess an organization's progress towards Excellence. Each of the nine criteria has a definition, which explains the high level meaning of that criterion. To develop the high level meaning further, each criterion is supported by a number of criterion parts. Criterion parts pose a number of questions that should be considered in the course of an assessment.

7.2   Relevance to IT management

The EFQM Excellence Model is a practical tool that can be used in a number of different ways:

- as a tool for self-assessment
- as a way to benchmark with other organizations
- as a guide to identify areas for improvement
- as a fundamental input to integrate with business planning and reviews
- as the basis for a common vocabulary and a way of thinking
- as a structure for the organization's management system

Frameworks for IT Management – A Pocket Guide

8 ISO 9000 – Quality Management Systems

International Organization for Standardization 9000:2000 (ISO 9000:2000) is a generic name given to a series of standards that have been developed to address the Quality Management Systems (QMS) within an organization, to demonstrate its capability to meet its customers' requirements.

8.1 Description and core graphics

ISO 9000:2000 is a single quality management requirements standard that is applicable to all organizations, products and services. It is not restricted to any particular layer of management and clearly defines the roles of each business area with regard to quality management.

ISO 9000 is made up of three sections:
- ISO 9000:2000 - QMS - fundamentals and vocabulary
- ISO 9001:2000 - QMS - requirements
- ISO 9004:2000 - QMS - guidelines for performance improvement

ISO 9000:2000 certifies that an organization has carried out the correct processes. It does not, however, provide a guarantee of the quality of the end product. Throughout the Standard the need for continuous improvement is heavily emphasized.

ISO 9000:2000 has four major generic business processes covering:
- the management of resources
- the quality of the product
- the maintenance of quality records
- the requirement for continual improvement

The aim of ISO 9000:2000 is to assist users in producing a QMS that is flexible, structured and customer-orientated.

ISO 9001:2000 and ISO 9004:2000 have been developed as a consistent pair of QMS standards based on eight quality management principles with a common process-oriented structure and harmonized terminology. They are designed to be used together, or may be used as standalone documents.

These eight principles (Figure 4) are of primary concern to any organization, as they will affect that organization's overall approach to quality. These principles:
• reflect best practice
• are designed to enable a continual improvement of the business and its overall efficiency
• are capable of responding to customer needs and expectations

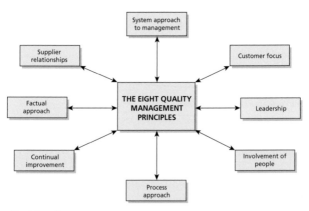

4 The eight quality management principles

ISO 9000:2000 is compatible with other internationally recognized management system standards, for example those dealing with environmental management, and with occupational health and safety. ISO 9000:2000 does not include any requirements that are specific to these other management systems. However, it does allow an organization to align and integrate its QMS with other management system requirements.

ISO has a set of guidelines to assist in the implementation of ISO 9001:2000 in the software sector (ISO/IEC 90003:2004 Software engineering, Guidelines for the application of ISO 9001:2000 to computer software). These guidelines provide support for organizations in the application of ISO 9001:2000 to the acquisition, supply, development, operation and maintenance of computer software and related support services. ISO/IEC 90003:2004 does not change the requirements of ISO 9001:2000 and its guidelines are not intended to be used as assessment criteria for registration/ certification.

ISO/IEC 90003:2004 is appropriate to software which is:
• part of a commercial contract with another organization
• a product available for a specific market sector
• a product used to support an organization's processes
• a product embedded in a hardware product or related to software services

Some organizations may be involved in all the above activities; others may specialize in one area. Whatever the situation, the organization's QMS should cover all aspects (software related and non-software related) of the business. ISO/IEC 90003:2004 identifies the issues which should be addressed and is independent of the technology, lifecycle models, development processes, sequence of activities and organizational structure used by an organization.

8.2   Relevance to IT management

ISO 9000:2000 is relevant to all organizations, products and services. It is therefore not specifically relevant to IT management. However, if there is a problem with the quality of the system, work will often need to be redone. This leads to a loss of productivity and wasted resources. Implementation of a quality management system can mitigate against this. Moreover, an organization which has already implemented ISO 9000:2000 will need considerably less effort to gain ISO 20000 certification.

9 ISO/IEC 20000 – ITSM standard

> *ISO/IEC 20000 is a formal standard for IT Service Management.*

9.1 Description and core graphics

ISO/IEC 20000 is recognized worldwide as the management standard for IT Service Management, addressing the establishment and maintenance of processes, and the mechanisms to ensure their relevance and improvement. Gaining certification against ISO/IEC 20000 is relevant to any service provider who wishes to demonstrate conformance with best practice in IT Service Management.

The requirements of the standard are owned and maintained by the International Organization for Standardization (ISO). Many national standards bodies publish the content of the standard with additional relevant content such as bibliography and compliance statements.

To get formal certification against ISO/IEC 20000, an organization has to be audited by a recognized certification body against an agreed scope. The scope must encompass all areas of the standard.

The standard comprises two parts:
- **Part 1 - Specification**: these are the documented requirements that an organization must comply with in order to achieve formal certification against ISO/IEC 20000, the 'shalls'
- **Part 2 - Code of Practice**: expansion, explanation, guidance and recommendations on the requirements of Part 1, the 'shoulds'

In general, Part 1 of the standard contains a list of mandatory controls: 'shalls' that service providers must comply with, in order to get certified.

Whereas, Part 2 contains a list of guidelines and suggestions that 'should' be addressed by service providers wishing to be certified.

Both parts share a common structure:

1. scope
2. terms and definitions
3. requirements for a management system
4. planning and implementing service management
5. planning and implementing new or changed services
6. Service Delivery processes
7. relationship processes
8. resolution processes
9. control processes
10. release process

The relationships of the key processes are illustrated in Figure 5.

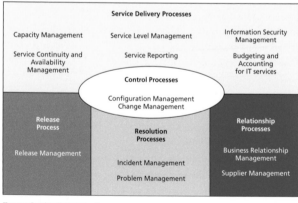

Figure 5 Service Management processes

As Figure 5 shows, there are four kinds of key processes that are all related to the fifth kind - the control processes. For all processes there are a defined objective and specifications.

The Service Delivery processes are:
- service level management
- service reporting
- service continuity and availability management
- budgeting and accounting for IT services
- capacity management
- information security management

The relationship processes are:
- business relationship management
- supplier management

The resolution processes are:
- incident management
- problem management

The control processes are:
- configuration management
- change management

The last process, the release process, is simply defined as the release management process.

Like any standard, ISO/IEC 20000 is primarily used as a demonstration of compliance to accepted best practice. In addition to the central elements of good IT Service Management best practice, it also requires service providers to implement the 'Plan-Do-Check-Act' methodology and apply it to their service management processes. This enshrines 'Continual Service Improvement' into the service provider. Thus, it ensures that the organization's processes develop, mature and adapt to their customers' requirements. Also, errors and omissions are avoided, and those that have been dealt with do not recur.

9.2 Relevance to IT management

ISO/IEC 20000 is appropriate to IT service provider organizations. It is appropriate to all industry sectors and to all sizes of organizations, though, for some very small service providers, the benefits of formal certification may not justify the costs of gaining and maintaining the standard.

An organizations' major objective in achieving ISO 20000 is the demonstration that they comply with the requirements set out in the standard. This, in turn, may be for one or more reasons, such as:

- **a focus for internal achievement** - a concrete demonstration of relevant and appropriate processes and approach within the service provider
- **demonstrating compliance** - to show credibility to existing and/or potential customers
- **formal requirement set down by customers** - requiring their service provider to comply with formally accepted best practice
- **corporate policy** - that the organization as a whole complies with all appropriate international standards

In addition to the formal demonstration of compliance, many organizations use ISO/IEC 20000 internally as a basis for Continual Service Improvement, by measuring compliance against selected controls and setting targets for improvement. In this case, although compliance to the full standard is not yet achieved, improvements in service can be measured, demonstrating period by period improvements through application of the principles of the standard. These measurements can be performed internally or by using external consultants.

10 TOGAF™ – The Open Group Architecture Framework

The Open Group Architecture Framework (TOGAF™) is a method for developing the architecture of an enterprise. Accompanied with supporting tools, this method provides a comprehensive approach to the design, planning, implementation and governance of an enterprise information architecture. TOGAF identifies the following subsets of an enterprise architecture: business, application, data, and technology. The core of TOGAF is the Architecture Development Method (ADM) that lists the phases of the development process.

The TOGAF documentation exists of three major components:

- **Architecture Development Method (ADM)** - the underlying structure for architecture developement
- **Enterprise Continuum** - a set of architectures, building blocks and products
- **Resource Base** - a set of tools and techniques

The ADM section is detailed below.

10.1 Description and core graphics

The TOGAF framework and its supporting tools may be used freely by any organization that wishes to develop an enterprise architecture for its own use.

The Architecture Development Cycle (Figure 6) shows the ADM's basic structure that distinguishes nine different phases that provide a standardized way of analyzing, planning, developing and managing of architectural changes:

1. **Preliminary phase: Frameworks and principles** - define the framework and the architecture principles
2. **Phase A: Architecture vision** - define the scope and obtain approvals
3. **Phase B: Business architecture** - identify the gap between current and target architecture
4. **Phase C: Information system architectures** - develop target architectures
5. **Phase D: Technology architecture** - create detailed process description of the target technical architecture
6. **Phase E: Opportunities and solutions** - develop the implementation strategy and identify project to be undertaken
7. **Phase F: Migration planning** - develop the migration plan
8. **Phase G: Implementation governance** - provide architectural governance
9. **Phase H: Architectural change management** - establish procedures for managing changes

The ADM Architecture Requirement Management's task is to define a process that identifies, stores, and implements requirements in the relevant ADM phases.

TOGAF supports four architecture domains:
1. **Business architecture** - defines the organization's business strategy, governance, and key business processes
2. **Applications architecture** - provides the blueprint for the individual application systems and their interactions and relationships to the organization's core business processes
3. **Data architecture** - describes the structure of the organization's logical and physical data assets and all associated data management resources
4. **Technology architecture** - describes the capabilities of both software and hardware that supports the deployment of business, data, and application services (for example IT infrastructure, middleware, standards, etc)

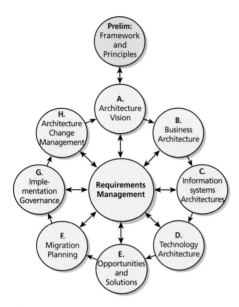

Figure 6 TOGAF Framework

TOGAF has been developed by The Open Group and is continuously
evolving ever since the mid-1990s. Currently, the latest TOGAF version
is the TOGAF 8.1 Enterprise Edition. TOGAF 9 is currently under
development.

10.2 Relevance to IT management

TOGAF is an architecture framework that enables IT users to design,
evaluate and build the right architecture for their organization. The key to
TOGAF is the practical Architecture Development Method (ADM) that
helps to define business needs and develop an architecture that meets those
needs.

TOGAF does not prescribe a specific set of 'architecture views', but offers example views for the architect to consider. In addition, it provides the guidelines for choosing and developing particular views.

The incorporation of governance into TOGAF makes that the framework aligns with the current business and ensures visibility and control that align with the stakeholder's requirements.

11 TickIT – Quality management for IT

TickIT was designed with and for the IT industry and includes practical guidance for both software development and service; as the TickIT guide's subtitle states: 'using ISO 9001:2000 for software quality systems construction, certification and continual improvement.'[1] A major element of TickIT is the scheme for certification of an organization's software quality management system to ISO 9001. TickIT is fully described in a public guide which contains detailed commentary on how to apply ISO 9001:2000 to software.

11.1 Description and core graphics

The TickIT Scheme was designed with and for the IT industry and covers software development, maintenance and service. At the core of TickIT is the third party certification scheme that is essentially a software sector implementation of ISO 9001 certification. TickIT also includes a published guidebook with the scheme rules, notes for purchasers and suppliers of software, as well as audit guidance to TickIT auditors.

TickIT can be used to support the development of all types of software, including operating systems, embedded systems or software for office use. It is based on ISO 9000-3 and adds information to the guidelines by providing additional guidance for customers, suppliers and auditors. It also contains clear requirements for auditors that must be met when accredited by certification bodies.

---

1   *The TickIT Guide: 'Using ISO 9001:2000 for software quality management system construction, certification and continual improvement'.* (2001, January, Issue 5.0.) London: British Standards Institution.

The certification aspects of the scheme are operated under the TickIT Uniform Arrangements which are based on well established national accreditation procedures. They are defined in the TickIT Guide and include the overall management of the scheme. The scheme is essentially ISO 9001 certification under long established and well known national accreditation arrangements. At present, national accreditation bodies in the UK (UKAS) and Sweden (SWEDAC) offer accreditation to certification bodies who want to offer TickIT services. As part of these uniform arrangements, TickIT auditors have to be registered with the International Register of Certificated Auditors (IRCA). Registration is by résumé, training and examination, and must be renewed every three years.

Figure 7 shows an example of the TickIT graphic that is used on certificates and marketing material.

Figure 7 TickIT graphic (Source: TickIT)

TickIT certification is relevant where software is developed and where the software is incorporated into the organization's delivered product or service.

Some examples of where it is used are:

• development of software products, whether application software, system software or embedded software

- delivery of systems/products where software is only a part of the included product
- internal software development for an organization's administrative systems
- facilities management and/or computer operations services where software development is part of the contract
- software replication services

11.2 Relevance to IT management

TickIT directly tackles the problems of poor quality and poor quality management in software.

The ISO 9001 Standard has specific requirements to monitor and measure processes and customer satisfaction. Once an organization has implemented these requirements, it should be able to assess the costs of poor software quality with a good degree of accuracy. This, in turn, will allow the quantification of benefits to be more easily expressed as the costs of poor software quality are driven down over time.

Successfully realizing a modern software quality management system means that the organization has defined, implemented and is managing a set of processes that are specifically suited for its purpose and goals. IT management thus gains increased visibility of the software development process; there is better management and control of the processes, and improved traceability between the processes and the associated quality controls.

12 ISO/IEC 19770 Software Asset Management

> *ISO/IEC 19770 is the international standard created for effective Software Asset Management (SAM). The standard is designed to provide support for IT departments to effectively manage processes and procedures and ensure compliance with legal and contractual requirement as well as corporate governance requirements. SAM should make management of business risks and cost control easier and offer competitive advantages.*

12.1 Description and core graphics

Organizations can use ISO/IEC 19770-1:2006 to form a structured baseline and to implement an integrated set of processes for Software Asset Management. The aim of the standard is to help organizations manage software more efficiently. Consequently, management and external organizations are confident of the quality and effectiveness of the organizations' processes.

The ISO/IEC 19770:2006 is a new standard that is still developing. It contains two parts:

- **ISO/IEC 19770–1** - describes the processes and procedures of software asset management.
- **ISO/IEC 19770–2** - this part is not published yet but is to define a product identification that simplifies the software inventory process.

ISO 19770 describes the guidelines in six main sections:

- **The control environment** - organizations need to use policies and procedures that outline the responsibilities in the Software Asset Management process.

- **Planning and implementation** - mapping of scope, required resources and policies, reporting structure, measurement and verification instruments. With implementation a continual improvement process needs to be in order.
- **Inventory** - Software Asset identification including auditable monitoring of its inventory.
- **Verification and compliance** - verification of Software asset records and matching of inventory to licenses. Includes authorization and optimizing license volumes.
- **Operations management** - security policy and document evidence of implementation, manage supplier relationships, and contracts (including maintenance of SLAs, contractual documents and budgets).
- **Lifecycle** - software assets lifecycle from change management and selection/acquisition/development of assets, incident management, problem management to retirement, transfer and disposals.

The standard is intended to align closely to and also support ISO/IEC 20000:2005. See Figure 8 for these relationships.

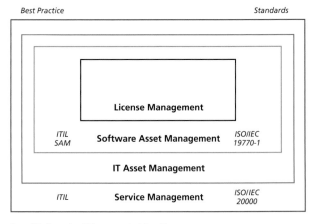

Figure 8 Software Asset Management relationships

Frameworks for IT Management – A Pocket Guide

12.2 Relevance to IT management

With the implementation of the ISO/IEC 19770-1:2006 standard, organizations are able to integrate Software Asset Management into their other compliance models and will allow them to benchmark their capability in delivering managed services.

The standard will help companies to manage their software assets and their licenses better. Applying the standard correctly can potentially save millions in license costs and maintenance fees every year.

13 ISO/IEC 15504 – SPICE

> *ISO/IEC 15504 (also known as SPICE (Software Process Improvement and Capability dEtermination) is the international standard for Software Process Assessment. ISO/IEC 15504 concentrates on the assessment of the software development process to ultimately lead to process improvement and to determine and improve software quality.*

13.1 Description and core graphics

ISO/IEC 15504 derives from ISO 12207 and provides a framework for consistent, reliable software process assessment. It consists of the following parts:

- Part 1 - Concepts and vocabulary
- Part 2 - Performing an assessment
- Part 3 - Guidance on performing an assessment
- Part 4 - Guidance on use for process improvement and process capability determination
- Part 5 - An exemplar process assessment model (for software lifecycle processes)
- Part 6 - An exemplar process assessment model for systems lifecycle processes (publication Q3 2007)
- Part 7 - Assessment of organizational maturity (expected publication 2008)

The 15504 standard focuses on software business processes such as: software development, project management, configuration management, quality assurance, etc.

ISO/IEC 15504 is complementary to the ISO 9001 (Table 2) model for quality assurance in design, development, production, installation and servicing. Further, ISO/IEC 15504 incorporates the goals of the ISO 9000 series:

• providing confidence in quality management
• providing acquirers with a framework that helps to assess whether potential suppliers have the capability to meet their needs

	ISO/IEC 15504	ISO 9001
Granularity	detailed model	abstract model
Focus	designed for software	designed for manufacturing, guidance for software
Purpose	process improvement and capability determination	certification
Scale	six capability levels, nine capability attributes	pass or fail
Guidance	requirements for assessment, guidance on application	model only
Integration	complementary to ISO 9001	complemented by ISO/IEC 15504

Table 2 Comparison ISO/IEC 15504 and ISO 9001

13.2 Relevance to IT management

ISO/IEC 15504 is used in the context of process improvement and capability determination. Process improvement and process capability determination processes are described in part 4 of ISO/IEC 15504.

Within the context of process improvement (PI), technology organizations can use ISO/IEC 15504 as the standard for assessing the organization's capabilities at each of the process stages. Outcome of the analysis of every stage will help list the strengths, weaknesses and risks that are related to the process. This way, the analysis will help to determine the effectiveness of the organizations processes in relation to their goals.

Process capability determination (PCD) can provide an organization with essential input about potential outsourcing suppliers. An technology organization that for example wants to outsource part of its software development can use the ISO/IEC 15504 framework to assess proposed suppliers.

Frameworks for IT Management – A Pocket Guide

14 ISO/IEC 27001 – Information Security Management Systems

ISO/IEC 27001 provides a model and detailed guidance for reducing an organization's exposure to information security risk, as implemented through an Information Security Management System (ISMS). Organizations will, in their lifetime, experience many changing information security risk profiles in the environment of their operations. An ISMS implemented under the ISO/IEC 27001 series of standards grows with the organization through planned maintenance and improvement cycles.

14.1 Description and core graphics

The ISO/IEC 27001 series of standards recognizes that many facets of information security management should be expressed through the implementation and operation of an ISMS. There are technical, human, system, organizational and societal factors, each of which contributes to the complexity of the topic, and a sophisticated and holistic approach is necessary to produce a 'fit for purpose' system (Table 3).

ISO/IEC 27001 has two parts:

- ISO/IEC 27001:2005, Information technology - Security techniques - Information Security management Systems - Requirements
- ISO 17799:2005, Information technology - Security techniques - Code of practice for information security management

ISO/IEC 27001:2005 provides a management approach to the synthesis of an information security management system that is 'fit for purpose', measured by the information security requirements and expectations of all interested parties.

ISO 17799:2005 is a code of practice, organized as 11 areas and 39 security control objectives, each of which is directed at a particular area of information security concern facing an organization. For each area, the code of practice describes high level information security objectives and the control by which risks in the scope of the objective are treated. Implementation guidance is also included.

ISO/IEC 27001:2005 includes a summary of ISO 17799:2005 in its Appendix.

Security area	High-level objective
Access Control	to control access to information
Asset Management	to achieve and maintain appropriate protection of organizational assets
Business Continuity Management	to counteract interruptions to business activities and to protect critical business processes from the effects of major failures of information systems or disasters, and to ensure their timely resumption
Communications and Operations Management	to ensure the correct and secure operation of information processing facilities
Compliance	to avoid breaches of any law, statutory, regulatory or contractual obligations, and of any security requirements
Human Resources Security	to ensure that employees, contractors and third party users: • understand their responsibilities and liabilities before during and after employment • are aware of security issues facing the organization and are equipped to deal with them in their normal duties • reduce the risk of theft, fraud, misuse of facilities, and human error
Information Security Incident Management	to ensure information security events and weaknesses associated with information systems are: • communicated in a manner allowing timely corrective action to be taken • dealt with in a consistent and effective manner

Security area	High-level objective
Information Systems Acquisition, Development and Maintenance	to ensure that security is an integral part of an installed information systems technology base
Organizing Information Security	to manage information security within the organization
Security Policy	to provide management direction and support for information security in accordance with business requirements and relevant laws and regulations

Table 3 Security areas and high level objectives

14.2 Relevance to IT management

The ISO/IEC 27001 series of standards is a key factor in IT management for any organization. Through the standard is recognized the value of information that an organization uses. Many of those information assets that are of value to an organization will be held on IT equipment, and many of the vulnerabilities that threaten to decrease their value exist because of IT equipment. Indeed, many of the controls chosen to manage the risks will impinge on IT management.

However, information security management is not just an IT management issue and treating it as such would be an error, because many of the information security vulnerabilities that are faced by organizations do not reside in the IT infrastructure, but in the social side of the organization's socio-technical system. Asset identification and risk assessment stages should thus be organization-wide.

On the control of risks side, many of the controls in the standard affect the management of IT, and their review and maintenance - a necessary component of the ISMS - will properly come within that function.

Frameworks for IT Management – A Pocket Guide

15 CMMI

CMMI-DEV, V1.2; (Capability Maturity Model® Integration for DEVelopment) is a process improvement maturity model for the development of products and services. It consists of best practices that address development and maintenance activities that cover the product lifecycle from conception through delivery and maintenance.

15.1 Description and core graphics

In 2002 version 1.1 of the CMMI was released as the successor of the CMM that was developed from 1987 until 1997. In 2006 the CMMI-DEV, CMMI for Development followed.

CMMI strives to give guidance in improving the organization's processes, to manage the development, acquisition and maintenance of products or services. CMMI uses best practices to form a structure that can help organizations to ensure mature process capabilities, with setting improvement priorities and implementing these improvements.

15.1.1 Representations: Continuous or Staged

The basic building blocks in every CMMI model are called 'process areas'. A process areas does not describe how an effective process is executed (for example entrance and exit criteria, roles of participants, resources). Instead, a process area describes the practices and goals of effective processes.

Each process area has specific goals. In the continuous representation of a CMMI model there are also generic goals.

In a Capability Maturity Model, a process area can be organized into one of two representations that differ on an organizational level (Figure 9):

- **Staged representation** - defines five maturity level components to measure process improvement. Each maturity level stands for a step in the organization's capability to managing projects. The maturity levels are:

- – initial
- – managed
- – defined
- – quantitatively managed
- – optimizing

- **Continuous representation** - uses process areas components to measure process improvement. The continuo us representation was also used in CMM, capability levels are defined for each level. A capability level consists of a generic goal and the generic practices related to a process area, which can improve the processes associated with that process area. The defined process areas are:

- – incomplete process
- – performed process
- – managed process
- – defined process
- – quantitatively managed process
- – optimizing process

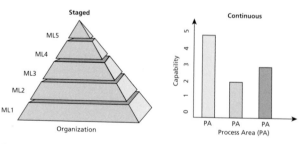

Figure 9 CMMI Overview, Staged vs. Continuous

Whether used for process improvement or appraisals, both representations are designed to offer essentially equivalent results.

15.2 Relevance to IT management

For the organizations that have IT as a competitive asset CMMI is useful as it becomes more and more important to put product on the market in a faster, better and more cost-effective way. Further, the development of software systems becomes increasingly complex and IT organizations have to be able to plan and monitor these complex development processes.

Frameworks for IT Management – A Pocket Guide

16 Six Sigma

*Six Sigma (6σ) is a branding term, given to a structured, disciplined,
rigorous approach to process improvement. It is a methodology that provides
businesses with the tools to improve the capability of their business processes
and/or IT processes. This increase in performance and decrease in process
variation leads to defect reduction (Six Sigma literally means only 3.4
defects per million opportunities occurring) and vast improvement in profits,
employee morale and quality of product.*

16.1 Description and core graphics

Six Sigma provides the tools and techniques to baseline existing level
of service quality, quantify service improvement for ROI and sustain
improvement with ongoing measurement and reporting. Moreover, Six
Sigma brings focus on what's 'critical to quality' and eliminating defects.
Defects that:

• impact the customers
• cost money (impact business bottom line)

The sigma measure, σ, represents the standard deviation. Six Sigma
means six times sigma, indicating 3.4 defects per million opportunities
(DPMO), or having 99.9997% confidence of achieving specified results. A
greater sigma implies a lower expected Defects per Million Opportunities
(DPMO) for defect or error.

The fundamental objective of the Six Sigma methodology is the
implementation of a measurement-based strategy that focuses on process
improvement and variation reduction through the application of Six Sigma
improvement projects.

The practical goal of this is to increase profits by eliminating variability,
defects and waste that undermine customer loyalty. This can be achieved

in many industries and for many purposes, such as operational excellence (process), IT development and IT maintenance.

Six Sigma relies on tried and tested methods that have been available for decades and combines these to create a new and structured methodology. It discards a great deal of the complexity that characterizes Total Quality Management (TQM): there are more than 400 TQM tools and techniques.

Six Sigma takes a small subset of these methods and trains a small cadre of in-house technical leaders, known as Six Sigma Black Belts, to a high level of proficiency in the application of these techniques. Some of the methods used by Black Belts, including up-to-date IT, are highly advanced. The principles can, however, be used by normal process engineers.

Given the impact on customer satisfaction of even one error, many organizations are incentivized to aspire to Six Sigma level DPMO to ensure better customer retention.

Six Sigma can be perceived at three levels:
- **Metric** - 3.4 Defects Per Million Opportunities (DPMO); DPMO takes the complexity of product/process into account; this should be measured in Critical to Quality (CTQ) characteristics, and not the characteristics of the whole unit
- **Methodology:**
  - DMAIC (Define-Measure-Analyze-Improve-Control) - structured problem solving roadmap and tools; this is an improvement system for existing processes falling below specification and looking for incremental improvement (Figure 10)
  - DMADV (Define-Measure-Analyze-Design-Verify) - data driven quality strategy for designing product and processes; this is an integral part of a Six Sigma Quality Initiative
  - DFSS (Design For Six Sigma) - unlike the DMAIC methodology, the phases or steps of DFSS are not universally recognized or defined -

almost every company or training organization will define DFSS differently; a company might tailor to suit its business, industry and culture, or it might implement the version of DFSS used by the consulting company assisting in its deployment; DFSS is more of an approach than a defined methodology

- **Philosophy** - reduce variation in the business and take customer-focused, data-driven decisions; the philosophy of Six Sigma is to use the framework not only for the process improvement projects, but also for the complete operation of the business

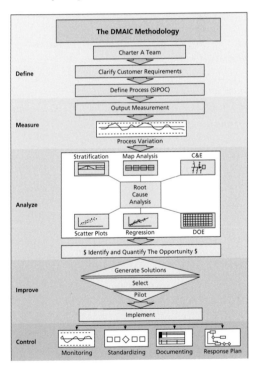

Figure 10 The DMAIC framework

16.2 Relevance to IT management

Six Sigma is a method that can be used to deliver tooling to optimize IT management. In this context Six Sigma is not used as a philosophy, but as a tool kit to solve IT management issues.

In IT management, many issues have a cause and effect relationship. Six Sigma can help with optimizing areas important to IT management, such as problem management, change management (for software) and software testing.

17 eSCM-SP v2: eSourcing Capability Model for Service Providers, version 2

The eSourcing Capability Model for Service Providers, version 2 – eSCM-SP v2 or SCM-SP – is a best practice framework that providers of IT-enabled services can use to develop and improve their ability to consistently deliver high quality services while minimizing costs and risks to their customers. The framework consists of a reference model, capability determination methods and a certification scheme.

17.1 Description and core graphics

The eSCM-SP is a capability model that defines the sourcing capabilities that service providers should develop and improve in order to be viewed by their current and prospective customers as capable and reliable partners. The sourcing capabilities are defined in terms of best practices that contribute to successful sourcing. These best practices are grouped into capability areas and structured into capability levels that describe the organizational capability of the service provider. The long-term proposition of the eSCM-SP is that sourcing relationships can be systematically managed to be more effective in delivering value and more resilient to business risks resulting from changes in economic and social conditions. The eSCM-SP Capability Determination Methods offer service providers a comprehensive and flexible approach to demonstrating value to both internal and external stakeholders.

The eSCM-SP v2 is composed of 84 practices that are considered useful
and relevant to achieving success in sourcing relationships. Each practice
has co-ordinates in a space defined by three dimensions, as shown in Figure
11:

1. sourcing lifecycle
2. capability area
3. capability level

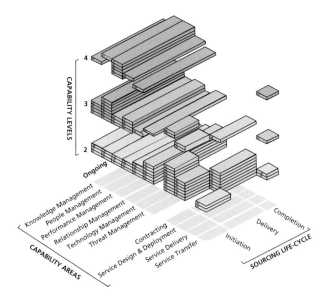

Figure 11 The structure of the eSCM-SP v2

17.1.1 Sourcing Lifecycle

In the first dimension, sourcing lifecycle, a practice can be one of the
following types:

• ongoing
• initiation

- delivery
- completion

17.1.2 Capability area

The second dimension of the eSCM-SP is defined in terms of capability areas that are logical groupings of practices to help users of the model better remember and intellectually manage its content. These groupings allow service providers to build or demonstrate capabilities in each critical sourcing function and map to the critical sourcing issues previously identified. The ten capability areas of eSCM-SP are:

- knowledge management
- people management
- performance management
- relationship management
- technology management
- threat management
- contracting
- service design and deployment
- service delivery
- service transfer

17.1.3 Capability levels

The third dimension of the eSCM-SP is defined in terms of capability levels. The five capability levels of the eSCM-SP describe an improvement path that customers should expect service providers to follow.

The five capability levels of the eSCM-SP are:

- Level 1: providing services
- Level 2: consistently meeting requirements
- Level 3: managing organizational performance
- Level 4: proactively enhancing value
- Level 5: sustaining excellence

17.2 Relevance to IT management

By definition, the eSCM-SP focuses on the work of service providers of IT-enabled services, where IT is a key component of service delivery or an enabler for delivering services. These services are often provided remotely, using telecommunication or data networks. They range from routine and non-critical tasks that are resource-intensive and operational in nature to strategic processes that directly affect revenues.

The eSCM-SP will be useful to service organizations seeking to evaluate, develop and improve their capabilities in the design, deployment and delivery of IT-enabled services, as well as helping them manage risks associated with sourcing contracts during the initiation and completion phases. Due to its focus on sourcing contracts, phases, relationships and operations, the eSCM-SP chooses to emphasize certain challenges and issues that, while faced by most organizations, are particularly critical for organizations that are engaged in the sourcing and provision of IT-enabled services.

18 IT Balanced Scorecard – the management system for strategic performance and results

> *The IT Balanced Scorecard is an instrument that can be leveraged to measure and manage IT performance and to enable alignment between the business and IT.*

18.1 Description and core graphics

The Balanced Scorecard is a performance management system that enables businesses to drive strategies based on measurement and follow-up. It was initially developed at enterprise level by Kaplan and Norton. The Balanced Scorecard can, however, easily be applied to information technology (IT) investments, projects or departments as an IT performance management and alignment instrument.

The fundamental premise of Kaplan and Norton is that the evaluation of an organization should not be restricted to a traditional financial evaluation, but should be supplemented with objectives and measures concerning customer satisfaction, internal processes and the ability to innovate. Results achieved within these additional perspective areas should assure future financial results and drive the organization towards its strategic goals while keeping all four perspectives (financial, customer, business process and learning and growth perspective) in balance.

For each of the four perspectives of the business Balanced Scorecard, Kaplan and Norton propose a three layered structure, as shown in Figure 12:

- **mission** - for example, to become the customer's preferred supplier
- **objectives** - for example, to provide the customers with new products
- **measures** - for example, the percentage of turnover generated by new products

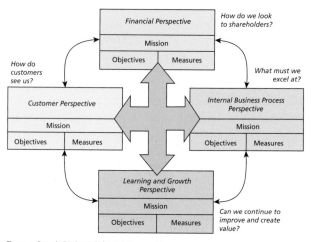

Figure 12 Generic Business Balanced Scorecard[2]

To leverage the IT Balanced Scorecard as a management and alignment instrument, it should be enhanced with 'cause and effect' relationships between measures.

---

2 Kaplan, R., & D. Norton (1992). The Balanced Scorecard – measures that drive performance. *Harvard Business Review, January-February, p. 71-79.*

These relationships are articulated by two types of measures:
- outcome measures (lag indicators)
- performance drivers (lead indicators)

A well developed scorecard should contain a good mix of these two metrics. Outcome measures without performance drivers do not communicate how they are to be achieved. And performance drivers without outcome measures may lead to significant investment without a measurement indicating whether the chosen strategy is effective.

18.2 Relevance to IT management

Getting business value from IT, and measuring that value, are important governance domains. These are responsibilities of both the business and IT, and should take both tangible and intangible costs and benefits into account. In this way, good IT performance management should enable both the business and IT to fully understand how IT is contributing to the achievement of business goals, in the past and in the future. Measuring and managing IT performance, for which the Balanced Scorecard is an ideal instrument, should provide answers to questions such as:
- If I spend extra funds on IT, what do I get back?
- How does my IT benchmark against competitors?
- Do I get back from IT what was promised?
- How do I learn from past performance to optimize my organization?
- Is my IT implementing its strategy in line with the business strategy?

Frameworks for IT Management – A Pocket Guide

19 AS 8015-2005 – Australian Standard for Corporate Governance of IT

The Australian Standard Corporate Governance of Information and Communication Technology (AS 8015-2005) provides a model, principles and vocabulary to assist those seeking to implement effective governance of the use of IT within their organizations.

19.1 Description and core graphics

AS 8015 Corporate Governance of Information and Communication Technology provides a framework for effective governance of the use of IT by an organization.

The standard defines corporate governance as the system by which entities are directed and controlled; a director as a member of the most senior governing body of an organization and an entity as a legally constituted organization.

AS 8015 provides a prudent approach to investment in IT, an approach which recognizes that there are risks associated with the operational and planned use of IT and ensures these are managed effectively.

The standard provides guidance to directors to help them meet their responsibilities in regard to IT and meet their obligations in relation to:

- privacy legislation
- record keeping
- financial reporting
- prudent management of organizational resources

The standard uses the term 'directors' to include owners, members of supervisory boards, partners, council members, senior executives, officers authorized by Acts of Parliament - in short, anyone responsible for the activities of an organization.

The framework described in AS 8015 comprises:
- a model
- guiding principles
- vocabulary

19.1.1 The model

Figure 13 reproduces the AS 8015 model. In the model, directors monitor and evaluate the organization's use of IT against the pressures and needs acting on it. They should then direct the development and implementation of policies and plans to address any gaps.

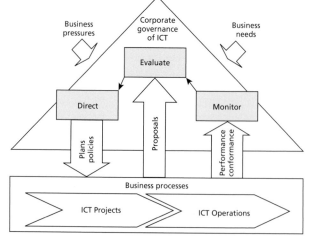

Figure 13 Model for corporate governance of IT (Source: AS 8015-2005 Australian Standard for Corporate Governance of Information and Communication Technology, Standards Australia)

Frameworks for IT Management – A Pocket Guide

19.1.2 Guiding principles

The standard provides six guiding principles:

- establish clearly understood responsibilities for IT
- plan IT to best support the organization
- acquire IT validly
- ensure that IT performs well, whenever required
- ensure IT conforms with formal rules
- ensure IT respec ts human factors

19.1.3 Vocabulary

The third component of the standard is a vocabulary drawn from, and complementing terms defined and used in, the other Australian Standards for corporate governance and risk management.

19.2 Relevance to IT management

AS 8015 provides a governance framework in which the use of IT can be managed and aligned to the organization's priorities.

The basis of the framework is to establish a framework for informed and timely decision-making on the use of IT, at the highest level of the organization.

For this to happen, appropriate measures and mechanisms need to be established for reporting and responding to the risks arising from the current or planned use of IT.

Frameworks for IT Management – A Pocket Guide

20 COBIT

> *Control Objectives for Information and related Technologies (COBIT) is a high-level process model that organizes a broad range of IT activities in 34 processes. As a single source of good practice it provides a uniform structure to understand, implement and evaluate IT capabilities, performance and risks with the primary goal of satisfying business requirements.*

20.1 Description and core graphics

COBIT is a globally recognized and adopted control-based, value and risk management framework used to support overall IT governance. COBIT is a flexible framework that needs to be aligned to an organization's business requirements.

COBIT provides managers, auditors, and IT users with a set of generally accepted measures, indicators, processes and best practices to assist them in maximizing the benefits derived through the use of IT and developing appropriate IT governance and control in a company (Figure 14).

The COBIT framework organizes IT activities in thirty four processes split into four domains:

- **Plan and Organize** - This domain covers the use of IT and how best it can be used in a company to help achieve the company's goals and objectives. It also highlights the organizational and infrastructural form that IT is to take, in order to achieve the optimal results and to generate the most benefits from the use of IT.
- **Acquire and Implement** - This domain covers identifying IT requirements, acquiring the technology, and implementing it within the company's current business processes. This domain also addresses the development of a maintenance plan that a company should adopt in order to prolong the life of an IT system and its components.

- **Deliver and Support** - This domain focuses on the delivery aspects of IT. It covers areas such as the execution of the applications within the IT system and its results, as well as the support processes that enable the effective and efficient execution of these IT systems.
- **Monitor and Evaluate** - This domain deals with a company's strategy in assessing the needs of the company and whether or not the current IT system still meets the objectives for which it was designed and the controls necessary to comply with regulatory requirements. Monitoring also covers the issue of an independent assessment of the effectiveness of IT system in its ability to meet business objectives and the company's control processes by internal and external auditors.

Related IT activities are collected within individual processes that are cross-referenced to provide an integrated set of IT processes with which to manage IT in line with business expectations.

At the process level there is a description of the outcomes to be expected (process goals) together with details about the minimum controls (detailed control objectives) to be considered in countering the inherent risks of that particular process, as well as a model to assess current capabilities (maturity model) to support the entity's business activities and described in relation to the people, technology and process details. CobiT 4.0 has included additional information about roles and responsibilities at the process level and the relationships between processes.

The detailed control objectives for each process provide some understanding of flow within the process and the essential controls. This can be used to understand the basic process and its controls. Additional detail about the process can be derived from the process specific maturity model and the more detailed Control Practice Statements – a separate publication from the main CobiT documentation set. The IT Control Practices expand the capabilities of the CobiT framework by providing the

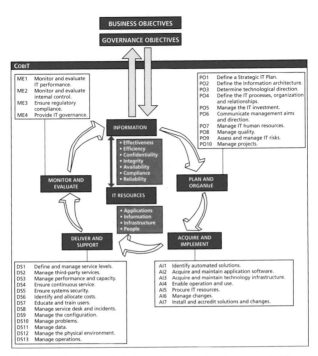

Figure 14 CoBiT IT processes defined within the four domains (Source: CoBiT 4.0, ISACA)

practitioner with an additional level of detail about how and why controls are needed by management, service providers, end users and control professionals.

At the activity level there are stated activity goals with the aim of making the process effective, key goal indicators to focus on the business expectations as well as Key Performance Indicators for managing the day-to-day activities.

20.2 Relevance to IT management

IT management can derive direct benefit from using the CobiT framework to implement better governance in three areas – building capability, directing IT activities with a view to achieving specific process outputs and measuring performance in successfully achieving outcomes that meet business goals.

Risk management, strategic alignment, value delivery, resource management and performance measurement will be improved through making use of the CobiT framework.

21 M_o_R – Management of Risk

> *Management of Risk (M_o_R®) is the overall process to assist in the effective control of risks. Risk can be defined as uncertainty of outcome, whether positive opportunity or negative threat, of actions and events. The risk has to be assessed in respect of the combination of the likelihood of something happening, and the impact which arises if it does actually happen.*

21.1 Description and core graphics

Every organization manages its risk, but not always in a way that is visible, repeatable and consistently applied to support decision-making. The task of Management of Risk (M_o_R) is to enable any organization to make cost effective use of a risk process that has a series of well defined steps. The aim is to support better decision-making through a good understanding of risks and their likely impact.

M_o_R provides a generic framework for the management of risk across all parts of an organization - strategic, program, project and operational. It incorporates all the activities required to identify and control the exposure to any type of risk, positive or negative, which may have an impact on the achievement of your organization's business objectives.

M_o_R is intended to help organizations to put in place effective frameworks for making informed decisions about risk. The guidance provides a route map for risk management, bringing together recommended approaches, checklists and pointers to more detailed sources of advice on tools and techniques. It expands on the OGC Guidelines for Managing Risk.

M_o_R covers a wide range of topics, including business continuity management, security, program/project risk management and operational service management. These topics are placed in the context of an organizational framework for the management of risk. Some risk-related topics, such as security, are highly specialized and this guidance provides only an overview of such aspects.

The process of investment appraisal, in which assessments are made of costs, benefits and risks, is outside the scope of this guide. However, many of the principles and techniques described here can be used when developing the business case.

M_o_R is enterprise-wide and can be applied to the three core elements of a business, namely (Figure 15):
• **Strategic** - business direction
• **Change** - turning strategy into action, including program, project and change management
• **Operational** - day-to-day operation and support of the business

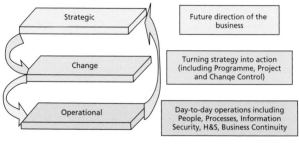

Figure 15 The three core elements of business where M_o_R can be applied (Source: OGC)

In this way, the strategy for managing risk should be led from the top of the organization while embedded in the normal working routines and activities of the organization.

While it is often misunderstood, even by risk managers, the aim of managing risk is not necessarily simply to reduce or eliminate risk within business, but to identify and manage risks to best effect for protecting and increasing shareholder value within the business. It has been stated that, paradoxically, better management of risk can allow an organization to take greater risks, but in a more controlled way, to the ultimate benefit of the organization and its shareholders.

21.2 Relevance to IT management

Within IT, every day risk is managed in relation to day-to-day operations and services to the business, programs and projects, disaster recovery and IT security.

By embedding the approach within the IT operation, IT management is more able to manage its risks through the visibility and reporting that would be in place.

One main challenge can be to ensure a 'no blame culture' within the organization, where staff and management are more willing to report on risks associated with their area of responsibility.

Frameworks for IT Management – A Pocket Guide

22 Generic Framework for Information Management

The Generic Framework for Information Management consists of three domains through which information problems can be considered: 'business', 'information and communication', and 'technology'. There are also three levels: strategy, structure and operations. They enable a more fine-tuned positioning of organizational problems.

Mainly, the framework concerns the distinction between the various strategic, structural and operational problems faced by information managers, and the distinction in technology, the significance of this technology and its application.

22.1 Description and core graphics

The Generic Framework for Information Management is a model for interrelating the different components of information management. It is used in the area of business-IT alignment and sourcing. It can be useful to consider IT governance issues as well. It is a high-level view of the entire field of information management; its main application is in the analysis of organizational and responsibility issues.

The framework is used to support strategic discussions in three different ways:

- **Descriptive, orientation** - The framework offers a map of the entire information management domain, to be used for positioning information management issues that are being discussed in the organization, whilst avoiding technical jargon.
- **Specifying, design** - The framework is used to re-organize the information management organization, such as specifying the role of the

Chief Information Officer (CIO), or determining the responsibility of the retained organization in the case of outsourcing.

- **Prescriptive, normative** - The map is used as a diagnostic instrument to find gaps in an organization's information management, specifically aimed at identifying missing interrelationships between the various components of the framework.

The model was derived from the Strategic Alignment Model from Henderson and Venkatraman. The Generic Framework for Information Management extends this model from a 2x2 matrix into a 3x3 matrix, by:

- replacing the external domains of (infra)structure and processes with the two tiers of structure and operations, resulting in a three-row framework: strategy, structure and operations
- adding a middle column representing the internal and external information and communication aspects, resulting in a three-column framework: business, information/communication and technology

The Generic Framework for Information Management is shown in Figure 16.

The framework provides some clarifying interpretations of information management:

- From the right to the left information is produced, interpreted and used. In the column at the right data is recognized, in the middle column information is recognized ('the interpretation of data') and in the left column knowledge is recognized ('making decisions based on information'). Information management relates to all three.
- For each of the three columns distinctive expertise is required (from the left to the right: business domain expertise, information expertise and technology expertise). Information management is primarily concerned with information expertise, but cannot do without the other two areas of expertise.

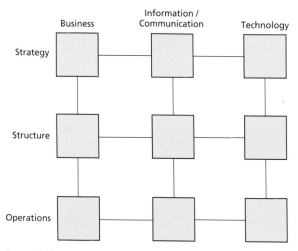

Figure 16 The Generic Framework for Information Management

- Technology introduces a new syntax, while the business column represents pragmatism. Therefore, it is the task of information management to provide practical meaning to this technology.

22.2 Relevance to IT management

The framework is especially important in the area of business–IT alignment. The intermediate structure row and information/knowledge/communication column are key to a successful alignment of business and IT. Hence, they should be considered as independent variables in their own right.

The framework primarily provides a reference frame for the positioning of information management issues at organization and/or business unit levels. From a normative point of view, the framework states that each of the nine areas and their mutual relations should be addressed. The central axes of the framework are core to information management.

Frameworks for IT Management – A Pocket Guide

23 ITIL version 3

ITIL (The IT Infrastructure Library) provides a framework of best practice guidance for IT Service Management that has become the most widely used and accepted approach to IT Service Management in the world. It has provided a universally accepted framework for establishing a set of integrated processes for delivering high quality IT services.

23.1 Description and core graphics

ITIL was originally developed by the Central Computer and Telecommunications Agency (CCTA, later to become part of the UK Office of Government Commerce (OGC)), in the late 1980s and early 1990s. The IT Infrastructure Library originated as a collection of books, each covering a specific practice within IT Service Management. After the initial publication, the number of books quickly grew within ITIL version 1, to 48 volumes.

In order to make ITIL more accessible (and affordable) to those wishing to explore it, one of the aims of ITIL version 2 (2000) was to consolidate the publications into logical 'sets' that grouped related process guidelines into the different aspects of IT management, applications and services.

The ITIL version 2 books and their disciplines were:
- service delivery
- service support
- ICT infrastructure management
- planning to implement service management
- application management
- the business perspective
- security management

In December 2005, the OGC issued notice of an ITIL refresh, commonly known as ITIL version 3. The ITIL refresh project ended with the publication of five new core texts and a web based glossary on 30th May 2007.

23.1.1 ITIL version 3 structure

The new ITIL structure is based on the idea that delivering IT services is of strategic value to the business and a strategic goal to the IT organization. Consequently, the Service Strategy is the basis around which the Service Lifecycle evolves (Design, Transition, Operation).

If you manage services through their lifecycle, it is logical that you learn how to do it better as you go along. This is where Continual Service Improvement comes in, touching on all the other phases and activities.

The way in which ITIL version 3 is now structured (when compared to ITIL version 2), switches from grouping the theory around specific fields of expertise (availability, incidents, etc) to grouping topics around the lifecycle of services.

The core of the ITIL Library consists of five publications. Each provides the guidance necessary for an integrated approach as required by the ISO/IEC 20000 standard specification:

- Service Strategy
- Service Design
- Service Transition
- Service Operation
- Continual Service Improvement

23.1.2 Service Strategy

Service Strategy explains how to design, develop and implement service management as an organizational capability and as a *strategic asset*. It shows how to develop service management policies, guidelines and processes

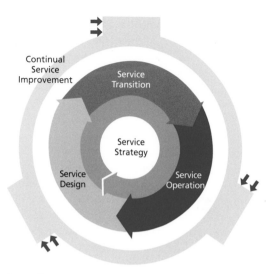

Figure 17 ITIL version 3

across the ITIL Service Lifecycle. Service Strategy sets the context for the other books. It includes the development of markets, internal and external, service assets, Service Catalogue and implementation of strategy through the Service Lifecycle. Financial management, Service Portfolio Management, organizational development and strategic risks are among the other major topics. It helps to answer the question '*why* something has to be done before thinking of the *how*'. Answers to the first type of questions are closer to the customer's business. Service Strategy expands the scope of the ITIL framework beyond the traditional audience of IT Service Management professionals.

The volume discusses the following topics:
- services and strategy
- financial management
- Return on Investment (ROI)
- Service Portfolio Management
- demand management
- strategy and organization

23.1.3 Service Design

Service Design deals with the design and development of services and
service management processes. It covers methods for converting strategic
objectives into portfolios of services and service assets. The scope of
Service Design is not limited to new services. It includes the changes
and improvements over the lifecycle of services, the continuity of
services, achievement of service levels, and conformance to standards and
regulations. It guides organizations on how to develop design capabilities
for service management. One trigger for this process is business process
change. Service Design starts as soon as the business requirements are clear.

The volume discusses the following topics:
- Service Catalogue Management
- Service Level Management
- capacity management
- availability management
- IT service continuity management
- information security management
- supplier management

23.1.4 Service Transition

Service Transition deals with capabilities for implementing new and
changed services. After setting a strategy and designing a service, this book
explains how the service can be effectively realized while controlling the
risks of failure and disruption. The book combines release management,

programme management and risk management in the practical context of service management. It shows how to manage the complexity of changes to services and service management processes. It also explains how to hand over control of services between customers and service providers.

The volume discusses the following topics:
- service assets
- utilities and warranties
- policies for Service Transition
- transition planning and support
- change management
- service asset and configuration management (SACM)
- release and deployment management
- service validation and testing
- evaluation
- knowledge management

23.1.5 Service Operation

Strategic objectives are ultimately realized through Service Operations, making it a critical capability. It helps to maintain stability in Service Operations, allowing for changes in design, scale, scope and service levels. It has detailed process guidelines, methods and tools for use in two control perspectives: reactive and proactive. It helps to make better decisions in managing the availability of services, controlling demand, optimizing capacity utilization, scheduling of operations and fixing problems. It supports operations with new models and architectures such as shared services, utility computing, web services and mobile commerce.

The volume discusses the following topics:
- event management
- incident management
- request fulfillment
- problem management

- access management
- operational activities of processes covered in other lifecycle phases
- common service operations activities
- Service Operation organization

23.1.6 Continual Service Improvement

This volume provides guidance in creating and maintaining value for customers through better design, introduction and operation of services. It combines principles, practices and methods from quality management, change management and capability improvement. Organizations learn to realize incremental and large-scale improvements in service quality, operational efficiency and business continuity. Guidance is provided for linking improvement efforts and outcomes with Service Strategy, Design and Transition. A closed-loop feedback system, based on the P-D-C-A model specified in ISO/IEC 20000, is established and capable of receiving inputs for change from any planning perspective.

The CSI improvement process takes the following steps:
1. define what you should measure
2. define what you can measure
3. gather data
4. process data
5. analyze data
6. present and use the information
7. implement corrective action

23.2 Relevance to IT management

ITIL enables and encourages IT management to recognize that, no matter how good an organization is at providing IT services, it can always improve. It gives a robust framework for relating and aligning with the business and its requirements on an on-going basis. It also recognizes that there are many problems associated with the delivery of high quality

IT services, and gives advice on how these can be avoided. It provides solutions to many problems including:

- a lack of vision, direction and senior management commitment
- poor business alignment and focus on business requirements, impacts and priorities
- poor relationships and communication
- poor quality of service
- low levels of customer satisfaction
- repeated disruption and failure of IT services
- poor track record of delivering IT solutions and changes

A key change to ITIL under version 3 has been a focus on the integration of IT and 'the business', on the management of IT throughout the complete lifecycle, and on the importance of creating business value, rather than just the execution of processes.

Frameworks for IT Management – A Pocket Guide

24 BiSL – the Business Information Services Library

The Business Information Services Library (BiSL) is a public domain approach that offers guidance in the field of business information systems management: support of the use of information systems in the business processes, operational IT control and information management. BiSL consists of a framework of processes, supplemented by various publications and a periodically updated library of best practices. BiSL is used as a management tool to improve the performance of processes and departments in the field of business information systems management.

24.1 Description and core graphics

The aim of the BiSL framework is to build bridges between the business processes and IT and between operational business information administration and high level information management.

BiSL identifies processes at the following three levels:

- **Operations** - The implementation or operational processes involve the day-to-day use of information provision, and determining and effecting changes to the latter.
- **Management** - The management processes involve income, expenditure, planning, the quality of information provision and making arrangements with IT suppliers.
- **Strategy** - As part of the processes at the strategic level the nature of information provision is determined for the long-term, together with how its management should be structured.

Within these three levels the various processes are grouped into seven process clusters, three at the operational level, one at the managerial level and three at the strategic level.

24.1.1 Process clusters at the operational level
The following three process clusters can be found at the operational level:
- use management
- functionality management
- linking processes at the operational level

24.1.2 Process clusters at the management level
The managerial processes act as a bridge, linking the strategic and operational processes. These processes ensure comprehensive management of the implementation of information provision. Four different aspects of managing are dealt with:
- planning of time, timelines and capacity
- cost-effectiveness
- demands and needs
- contracts and service level agreements

24.1.3 Process clusters at the strategic level
These clusters involve the formulation of policy concerning information provision and the organizations related to this. The following three process clusters can be found at the strategic level:
- develop information strategy
- develop information organization strategy
- linking process at the strategic level

Figure 18 shows the overall BiSL framework.

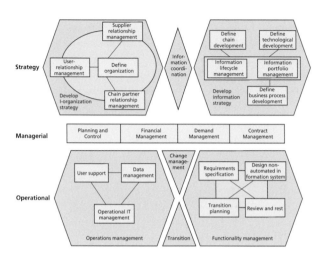

Figure 18 The overall BiSL framework

24.2 Relevance to IT management

In the last few years awareness of business information systems management has risen. The most important reasons for this are:

- **Growing importance of information provision** - Business processes and information provision have become more and more intertwined. Information provision becomes an important aspect of managing the business processes.

- **An increasing number of situations where IT is outsourced** - When outsourcing IT services the business organization needs to take control. It has to act like any other customer: stating demands, determining a fair price to pay for these demands and setting a long-term view on information provision.

- **Different parties involved and different demands** - Most organizations consist of several departments or other organizational parts that make use of common IT infrastructures and common information systems/ applications. However, these different departments may also have different and sometimes even opposing information demands. A clear and transparent structure is needed that is responsible for decision-making about information provision.

As the examples above show, business information systems management is becoming more and more important. The BiSL framework helps organizations to put their business information management processes in place.

25 ISPL – the Information Services Procurement Library

The Information Services Procurement Library (ISPL) is a systematic approach to tendering and delivering IT projects and services. Its main purpose is to professionalize customer-supplier relationships.

25.1 Description and core graphics

ISPL is a 'Best Practice' for acquiring of IT related services. It offers a set of books, tools and services to help customer and supplier organizations to manage the acquisition and delivery of services and systems in a variety of situations.

It encourages customers and suppliers to control costs and timescales, manage risks and improve mutual understanding. Lots of services and projects now fail due to inadequate risk management. The approach offered is, in particular, beneficial to analyze and manage the underpinning complexity and uncertainty.

ISPL has been developed for use in both the public and the private sector. It is mainly used in large-scale services, but its recommendations are also useful in small-scale services.

Two processes are focal within ISPL: the acquisition process and the procurement process. Acquisition processes aim at acquiring IT related systems and services (see Figure 19).

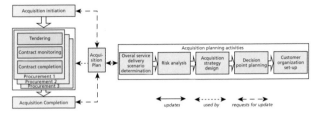

Figure 19 The acquisition process (Source: ISPL consortium)

The customer organization initiates the acquisition process by determining:
- **the acquisition goal** - which systems and services to be acquired
- **the acquisition strategy** - how many suppliers, which procurement, how to engage with suppliers, how flexible should the contracts be, and so on

Initiation of the acquisition process is followed by one or more procurement processes. Finally, the acquisition process is completed.

Procurement processes aim at preparing a contract and subsequently acquiring the deliverables and services defined in that contract (see Figure 20). Procurement processes consist of a tendering process, a contract monitoring process and a contract completion process.

The right halves of both Figure 19 and Figure 20 show a set of activities that can be executed throughout acquisition and procurement processes, emphasizing risk analysis, strategy design and decision point planning. ISPL provides guidance and heuristic teaching for these activities. To be in control of these processes, two deliverables have been designed; the acquisition plan and the delivery plan. ISPL offers guidance to produce these deliverables, among others, by a number of predefined activities. Risk analysis, the design of the delivery strategy and the planning of decision points are examples of those activities.

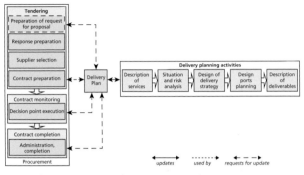

Figure 20 The procurement process (Source: ISPL consortium)

25.2 Relevance to IT management

This instrument is specifically relevant to IT management, as there is a strong focus on understanding and managing large-scale, complex, uncertain IT requirements.

The major benefits of using ISPL for customer organizations are:
- formulating clear IT requirements
- designing a delivery strategy that is customized to the critical risks
- designing an acquisition strategy that is customized to the critical risks
- organizing decision-making processes in a transparent way
- receiving comparable suppliers' responses
- gaining advantage from a competitive market

The major benefits of using ISPL for supplier organizations are:
- formulating clear IT requirements
- designing a delivery strategy that is customized to the critical risks
- designing an acquisition strategy that is customized to the critical risks
- organizing decision-making processes in a transparent way
- understanding customers' responsibilities

All these benefits contribute to professional customer-supplier relationships.

26 eTOM – the enhanced Telecom Operations Map

The enhanced Telecom Operations Map (eTOM) is the most widely used and accepted standard for business process in the telecom industry. The eTOM describes the full scope of business processes required by a service provider and defines the key elements and how they interact, creating a guidebook that is fast becoming the common business language of the telecom industry.

26.1 Description and core graphics

eTOM is the ongoing TM Forum initiative to deliver a business process model or framework for use by service providers and others within the telecommunications industry.

eTOM describes all the enterprise processes required by a service provider and analyzes them to different levels of detail according to their significance and priority for the business. For such companies, it serves as the blueprint for process direction and provides a neutral reference point for internal process re-engineering needs, partnerships, alliances and general working agreements with other providers.

For suppliers, eTOM outlines potential boundaries of software components to align with the customers' needs and highlights the required functions, inputs and outputs that must be supported by products.

The eTOM Business Process Framework represents the whole of a service provider's enterprise environment. The Business Process Framework begins at the Enterprise level and defines business processes in a series of groupings. The framework is defined as generically as possible so that it is organization, technology and service independent, and supports the global community. At the overall conceptual level (see Figure 21), eTOM can be viewed as having the following three major process areas:

- **Strategy, Infrastructure & Product** - covering planning and lifecycle management
- **Operations** - covering the core of operational management
- **Enterprise management** - covering corporate or business support management

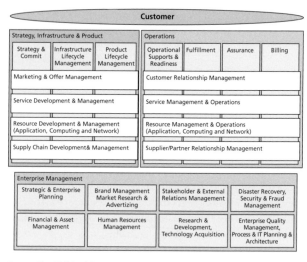

Figure 21 The eTOM Level One process map

The process structure in eTOM uses hierarchical decomposition, so that the business processes of the enterprise are successively decomposed in a series of levels. Process descriptions, inputs and outputs, as well as other key elements are defined. The eTOM process modeling depicts process flows in a vertical swim lane approach that drives end-to-end process and process flow-through between the customer and the supporting services, resources and supplier/partners.

The framework also includes views of functionality as they span horizontally across an enterprise's internal organizations. For example, managing customer relationships spans an enterprise from marketing to ordering to billing to after-service support and follow-on sales.

26.2 Relevance to IT management

IT is one of the main drivers for the next generation of telecommunication services, so that not only the network but also a significant amount of IT has to be managed, in order to provide innovative and new service offerings while maintaining a high level of flexibility and responsiveness to change. These changes are not only visible in the technology domain, but also in the commercial and in the regulatory domains; they require the flexibility of a modular approach for processes and the associated IT support, which can be found in the levels and in the end-to-end processes of the eTOM model. This process modularity provides clear separations between areas of responsibility, for example, between business management logic and service management logic.

The eTOM Business Process Framework can be used as a tool for analyzing the organization's existing processes and for developing new processes. Different processes delivering the same business functionality can be identified, duplication eliminated, gaps revealed, new process design speeded up, and variance reduced. Using eTOM, organization's can assess the value, cost and performance of individual processes within the organization.

Frameworks for IT Management – A Pocket Guide

27 ASL – the Application Services Library

> The Application Services Library (ASL) is a public domain approach for
> management, maintenance and enhancement/renovation of (business)
> applications. It consists of a framework of processes, supplemented by
> various publications and a periodically updated library of best practices.
> Organizations use ASL as a management tool to improve the performance of
> application management services.

27.1 Description and core graphics

ASL is a framework and library of best practices in the field of application
management.

The ASL Framework includes generic process descriptions of all the
26 processes, including items such as goal, input/activities/output and
relationships with the other processes (Figure 22). The framework consists
of six process clusters, divided into three levels: the operational and
management processes have a short to medium term perspective, whereas
the governance processes look two years ahead.

27.1.1 Maintenance and control cluster

This cluster aims to ensure that the current applications are used in the
most effective way to support the business processes, using a minimum
of resources, and leading to a minimum of operational interruptions. The
five processes are similar to ITIL processes with the same names and with
similar objectives, but with different content, due to the different nature of
application management.

27.1.2 Enhancement and renovation cluster

This cluster ensures that the applications are modified in line with
changing requirements, usually as a result of changes in the business

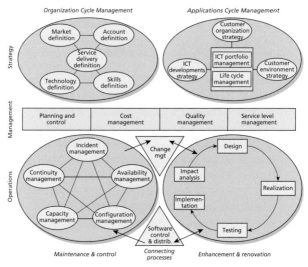

Figure 22 ASL Framework

processes, keeping the applications up-to-date. These processes are similar to activities performed during the initial development of applications.

27.1.3 Connecting processes

The operational process clusters maintenance and control and enhancement and renovation are closely related, as they deal with the same application objects. The two connecting processes deal with transferring software and data enhancement to maintenance in a controlled way:

- change management
- software control and distribution

27.1.4 Management processes

The management processes ensure that all of the operational process clusters are integrally managed. Attention is paid to managing human resources, deadlines, revenue and costs, and internal and external quality (service levels).

27.1.5 Applications Cycle Management (ACM)

This process cluster deals with business and IT alignment, developing a long-term strategy for the information systems, in line with the long-term strategies of the (business) organization. It is approached from two perspectives: the individual applications and the application portfolio, looking at all the applications in relation to each other.

27.1.6 Organization Cycle Management (OCM)

This process cluster looks at the long-term organizational development of the application management unit, whether this is an internal department or a commercial organization. OCM stipulates that the application management department or company considers not only its customers' future needs but also its own future.

Based on the ASL framework and best practice with application management, an ASL maturity model was developed, to measure the maturity of individual processes and of the application management services organization.

27.2 Relevance to IT management

IT management is faced with a number of major challenges: justifying the large proportion of IT spending, mitigating operational and other risks while coping with increasing technical and organizational complexity and the seemingly never-ending challenge of bridging the gap between IT and the business.

ASL can make a contribution to resolving these issues by providing more insight into the costs of application management, reducing risks by improving the reliability of both management processes and operational processes and finally improving the alignment with the business by initiating and feeding a strategic dialogue between application management and business information management.

28 MSP – Managing Successful Programmes

> *The method 'Managing Successful Programmes' (MSP) is a systematic approach to manage successful programs to achieve outcomes and realize benefits that are of strategic importance.*

28.1 Description and core graphics

MSP describes the best practice to manage programs. It adopts a process model of initiating, defining, governing and closing a program (Figure 23). It also contains seven knowledge areas, known as 'principles':

- organization and leadership
- benefits management
- stakeholder management and communications
- risk management and issue resolution
- program planning and control
- business case management
- quality management

These principles represent the skills and practices that the program management team will need. The method is then supported by a glossary of program management terms, a risk identification checklist and product description outlines for the most important program management documents.

28.1.1 Program management lifecycle

The initiative to start a program can come from any level in the organization, but it is only viable if supported by senior management. This starts with the program mandate to the future senior responsible owner. In order to clarify the scope of the program, the senior responsible owner will first set up a program brief (for identifying the program) for approval by the sponsoring group.

Following approval, a program team, led by the program manager and based on the program brief, will prepare the program definition with the associated plans, strategies and risk and issues registers for managing the program (*defining a program*).

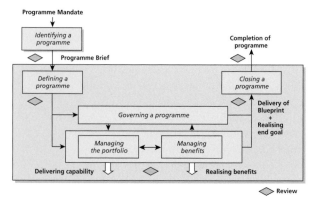

Figure 23 Program processes and main products (Source: Program Management based on MSP)

Implementation of the program can start following review and approval of the program definition and all plans, strategies and risk and issues registered by the sponsoring group at the end of defining a program. First, program control and a program office must be set up. The program must be managed and its performance assessed throughout the entire process (governing the program).

New projects are started up. Existing projects with program objectives are aligned. The program portfolio of projects is co-ordinated and monitored in accordance with the program plan and adjusted for the constantly changing environment (managing the portfolio).

The departments concerned must be prepared for the changes, and the new capabilities are implemented. The envisaged benefits are realized. The new way of working should be embedded into the organization in order to become the new 'business as usual' (managing benefits).

The program should be closed, either once the end goals have been achieved, or when the required new or revised capabilities described in the blueprint have been delivered, and it has been concluded that the remaining benefits to be realized do not require a separate program organization any more. The program is given a final assessment, the organization disbanded and the responsibility for the realization of the remaining benefits and the associated performance measurements transferred to the respective departments (*closing a program*).

28.2 Relevance to IT management

MSP provides organizations with an approach to program management that will:

- enable more effective delivery of change
- keep the focus on the business change objectives
- provide a framework for senior management to direct the change process
- encourage more efficient use of resources through project prioritization and integration
- provide better management of risk because the wider context is understood
- achieve business benefits during and after the program through a formal process
- improve control of costs, standards and quality
- enable more effective management of the business case
- provide more efficient control of a complex range of activities
- provide clear definition of roles and responsibilities
- deliver a smooth transition from current to future business operation

29 PRINCE2 – PRojects IN Controlled Environments

> *PRINCE2 (PRojects IN Controlled Environments) is a project management method for any type of project. It has been derived from professional project managers' experiences and refined over years of use in a wide variety of contexts.*

29.1 Description and core graphics

PRINCE2 is a scalable, flexible project management method, suitable for use on any type and any size of project. For smaller projects, though, not all processes and documents need to be applied, but only those that are absolutely necessary for the given circumstances and that provide added value for the organization and management of that project.

There are two key principles of PRINCE2:
- A project should be driven by its business case
- PRINCE2 is product-based

A key approach of the method is that it firmly distinguishes the management of the development process from the *techniques* involved in the development process.

The method consists of eight *processes*, eight components and three *techniques*. Figure 24 shows how they fit into the 'big picture' of the PRINCE2 method.

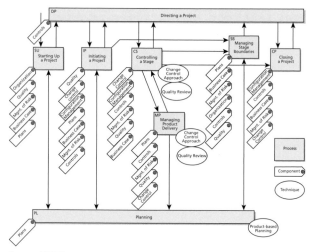

Figure 24 PRINCE2 processes, components and techniques

29.1.1 Processes

PRINCE2 offers a set of processes that provide a controlled start, controlled progress and a controlled close to any project:

- starting up a project
- initiating a project
- directing a project
- controlling a stage
- managing product delivery
- managing stage boundaries
- closing a project
- planning

The processes explain what should happen, when it should be done and by which role. Any project run under PRINCE2 will need to address each of these processes in some form. However, the key to successful use of the process model is in tailoring it to the needs of the individual project. Each process should be approached with the question: 'How rigorously should this process be applied on this project?'

29.1.2 Components

PRINCE2 has eight components to explain its philosophy about various project aspects. The eight components include:

- business case
- organization
- plans
- controls
- management of risks
- quality in a project environment
- configuration management
- change control

This philosophy is implemented through the processes.

29.1.3 Techniques

PRINCE2 offers three techniques. The use of most of them is optional:

- product-based planning
- quality review technique
- change control technique

The organization may already have a technique that is covering a requirement satisfactorily, such as quality checking and change control. PRINCE2 works effectively alongside such in-house techniques. The exception is the product-based planning technique. Product-based planning is fundamental to PRINCE2. There are two reasons for this: Firstly a project delivers products, not activities, so why begin at a lower level? The second reason concerns quality. The quality of a product can be measured. The quality of an activity can only be measured by the quality of its outcome (the product).

Product-based planning has three components:
- product breakdown structure
- product descriptions
- product flow diagram

29.2 Relevance to IT management

As the method was originally devised for IT by a group of IT managers, it is still very relevant to the management of IT projects. It has an excellent approach to the planning and organization of a project and describes the production of a business case, often a weak area in IT projects. The 'closing a project' stage is also very relevant as many IT staff are more interested in moving on to the next innovative project, rather than formally closing down a project and tying up any loose ends. The concept of a work package 'contract' between the project manager and a team manager brings a discipline often lacking in IT projects.

30 PMBoK – the Project Management Body of Knowledge

The project management Body of Knowledge (PMBoK®) is a document guide gathering knowledge, concepts, techniques and skills of the project management profession.

30.1 Description and core graphics

The Project Management Body of Knowledge (PMBoK) is a collection of processes and knowledge areas generally accepted as best practice within the project management discipline. As an internationally recognized standard (IEEE Std 1490-2003) it provides the fundamentals of project management, irrespective of the type of project, whether it is construction, software, engineering, automotive, etc.

PMBoK recognizes five basic process groups and nine knowledge areas which are typical of almost all projects. The basic concepts are applicable to projects, programs and operations.

The five basic process groups are:
- initiating
- planning
- executing
- controlling
- closing

Processes overlap and interact throughout a project or phase. Processes are described in terms of:

- inputs (documents, plans, designs, etc.)
- tools and techniques (mechanisms applied to inputs)
- outputs (documents, products, etc.)

The nine knowledge areas are:

- project integration management
- project scope management
- project time management
- project cost management
- project quality management
- project human resource management
- project communications management
- project risk management
- project procurement management

These areas represent the skills and practices that the project manager should gather (Figure 25).

30.2 Relevance to IT management

The PMBoK is an instrument that tries to solve common project problems, in an integral, consistent document, and a process of continuous improvement.

Much of PMBOK is unique to project management, such as critical path and work breakdown structure (WBS). Some areas overlap with other management disciplines. General management also includes planning, organizing, staffing, executing and controlling the operations of an organization. Financial forecasting, organizational behavior and planning techniques are also similar.

1. Project integration mgt.	2. Project scope mgt.	3. Project time mgt.
1.1 Develop project charter	2.1 Scope planning	3.1 Definition of activities
1.2 Develop preliminary project scope statement	2.2 Scope definition	3.2 Sequence of activities
1.3 Develop project mgt. plan	2.3 WBS creation	3.3 Estimation of activities resources
1.4 Direct and manage project execution	2.4 Scope verification	3.4 Estimation of activities duration
1.5 Monitoring and control project	2.5 Scope control	3.5 The development of the chronogram
1.6 Integrated change control		3.6 The control of the chronogram
1.7 Close project		

4. Project cost mgt.	5. Project quality mgt.	6. Project human resource
4.1 Estimation of costs	5.1 Quality planning	6.1 Human resources planning
4.2 Budget of costs	5.2 Quality security planning	6.2 Staff recruitment
4.3 Control of costs	5.3 Quality control execution	6.3 The Development of the team work
		6.4 The Team work management

7. Project Communications	8. Project risk mgt.	9. Project procurement mgt.
7.1 Communications planning	8.1 Identification of Risks	9.1 Purchase and acquisition Planning
7.2 Distribution of infomation	8.2 Risk management planning	9.2 Contracts planning
7.3 Reporting performance	8.3 Risk qualitative analysis	9.3 Response requirement salesman
7.4 Stakeholders management	8.4 Quantitative analysis	9.4 Selection of the salesman
	8.5 Risk response planning	9.5 Contract administration
	8.6 The Control of the risks	9.6 Contract closing

Figure 25 The nine areas and their processes (Source: PMBoK® Guide Third Edition 2004)

IT must add value to an organization; it must develop its competence in areas such as teamwork, negotiation, resolution of conflicts, communication, risks and in the definition of effective processes. These competences are presented in the PMBoK in the form of a body of knowledge that unifies processes, knowledge, necessary skills and techniques for the management of projects.

IT projects are becoming of greater importance and visibility, for which professional project management is essential. The PMBoK with its modern approach, supported by specialist knowledge in all the major industry sectors, contributes to this professional approach.

Another aspect to emphasize is that the recognition of PMBoK as an ANSI standard means that it can be referenced as the project approach in response to Requests for Proposals (RFP) for IT projects.

31 IPMA Competence Baseline

The IPMA Competence Baseline (ICB) is the competence standard for project management and is not restricted to any sector or branch. It was issued by the International Project Management Association (IPMA) as the common framework document which all IPMA Member Associations and Certification Bodies conform to, to ensure consistent and harmonized standards for certification are applied. As such, the majority of its content focuses on the description of the project management competence elements.

31.1 Description and core graphics

The ICB defines forty six competence elements covering the technical competence for project management (twenty elements), the professional behavior of project management personnel (fifteen elements), and the relationships with the context of the projects, programs and portfolios (eleven elements). The complete listing is shown in Table 4.

Each competence element consists of a title, a description of the content, a list of possible process steps and experience criteria required for each IPMA certification level. The key words and the key relationships to other elements are listed at the end of each element for comprehensive reading. The behavioral competences also contain pairs describing adequate behavior versus behavior that needs to improve.

The ICB does not recommend or include specific methodologies, methods or tools. Methods and tools may be defined by the organization. The project manager should choose appropriate methods and tools for a particular project situation.

Competences					
	Technical		**Behavioral**		**Contextual**
1.01	Project management success	2.01	Leadership	3.01	Project orientation
1.02	Interested parties	2.02	Engagement	3.02	Program orientation
1.03	Project requirements and objectives	2.03	Self-control	3.03	Portfolio orientation
1.04	Risk and opportunity	2.04	Assertiveness	3.04	Project, program and portfolio implementation
1.05	Quality	2.05	Relaxation	3.05	Permanent organization
1.06	Project organization	2.06	Openness	3.06	Business
1.07	Teamwork	2.07	Creativity	3.07	Systems, products and technology
1.08	Problem resolution	2.08	Results orientation	3.08	Personnel management
1.09	Project structures	2.09	Efficiency	3.09	Health, security, safety and environment
1.10	Scope and deliverables	2.10	Consultation	3.10	Finance
1.11	Time and project phases	2.11	Negotiation	3.11	Legal
1.12	Resources	2.12	Conflict and crisis		
1.13	Cost and finance	2.13	Reliability		
1.14	Procurement and contract	2.14	Values appreciation		
1.15	Changes	2.15	Ethics		
1.16	Control and reports				
1.17	Information and documentation				
1.18	Communication				
1.19	Start-up				
1.20	Close-out				

Table 4 The competence elements of ICB

IPMA defines four levels of competence.

1. At **IPMA Level A** the candidate must have demonstrated successful use of the competence elements in the co-ordination of programs and/or portfolios. The candidate has guided program and/or project managers in their development and in the use of the competence elements. The candidate has been involved in implementing the competence elements or relevant methodology, techniques or tools in projects or programs. The candidate has contributed to the development of the project manager's profession by publishing articles or presenting papers on their experiences or by outlining new concepts.

2. At **IPMA Level B** the candidate must have demonstrated successful use of the competence elements in complex project situations. The candidate has guided (sub) project managers in their application and implementation of the competence.

3. At **IPMA Level C** the candidate must have demonstrated successful use of the competence element in project situations with limited complexity. The candidate might need to be guided in further development of the competence element.

4. At **IPMA Level D** only knowledge related to the competence element is assessed (by written examination).

A large number of national and international organizations have adopted the IPMA certification to be the backbone of their project management competence development.

The ICB, together with the IPMA Certification Regulations and Guidelines (ICRG), documents the IPMA four-level certification. The certification system complies with the relevant ISO-standards 9001: 2000, ISO 10006 and ISO/IEC 17024: 2003.

The *benefits* of the certification programs are:
- **for project management personnel** - to obtain an internationally recognized certificate acknowledging their competence in project management
- **for the suppliers of project management services** - a demonstration of their employees' professional competence
- **for customers** - more certainty that they will receive high quality services from a project manager

The IPMA four-level certification can be used as a requirement in the selection and/or professional development of project management personnel.

31.2 Relevance to IT management

Working in projects is a way of life in IT and almost every significant business project contains IT sub-projects. Investing in mature projects and project management is essential for survival in the IT industry. Projects contribute substantially to business and IT alignment.

32 Company specific standards

A number of other IT Service Management frameworks have been developed on the basis of ITIL, generally by commercial organizations. Examples include Hewlett-Packard (HP ITSM Reference model), IBM (IT Process Model), Microsoft (MOF), Quint Wellington Redwood (IPW and IPW Stage Model), and many others. These models have been documented in several ITSM publications, but never in much detail (with the exception of MOF), since they are proprietary.

This is one of the reasons why ITIL has become the de facto standard for describing in detail a number of fundamental processes in IT Service Management. The adoption and adaptation of ITIL directly reflects the ITIL philosophy and is a welcome development, as ITIL has become a force for industry alignment that is sorely needed in todays heterogeneous and distributed IT environment.